I0137630

Understanding Karma and Rebirth

A Buddhist Perspective

Understanding Karma and Rebirth

A Buddhist Perspective

Diana St Ruth

Buddhist Publishing Group

Totnes

Buddhist Publishing Group
Totnes, England
www.buddhistpublishing.com

First published by Thorsons, an imprint of
HarperCollins Publishers, in 2002, as *Karma,
Reincarnation and Rebirth.*

Buddhist Publishing Group abridged edition 2008 and
this revised edition 2025

Copyright © Diana St Ruth 2002, 2008

Copyright © Diana St Ruth (Revised Edition) 2025

Diana St Ruth asserts the moral right to be identified as
the author of this work

A catalogue record for this book is available from the
British Library

ISBN 9780946672301

Cover photo: Sir John Aske, B.t.

All rights reserved. No part of this book may be
reproduced or stored in any form or by any means,
electronic, digital, or mechanical, including
technologies now known or later developed, without
written permission from the publisher.

I dedicate this book to my mother and grandmother.

Other titles by Diana St Ruth

An Introduction to Buddhism

Experience Beyond Thinking:
A Practical Guide to Buddhist Meditation

Little Book of Buddhist Wisdom, Compiled by
Richard and Diana St Ruth

Simple Guide to Theravada Buddhism, by
Richard and Diana St Ruth

Simple Guide to Zen Buddhism, by
Richard and Diana St Ruth

Contents

Nibbāna Sutta

'Thus have I heard: At one time, the Blessed One was staying at Sāvatthī, in Jeta's Grove, the monastery of Anāthapiṇḍika. At that time, the Blessed One (The Buddha) was instructing, inspiring, rousing, and gladdening the monks with a Dhamma talk related to Nibbāna. And those monks, having set their attention on the talk, focused their minds, and with attentive ears, listened to the Dhamma.

'Then, understanding the significance of this, the Blessed One, at that time, uttered this inspired utterance: "There is, monks, an unborn, unbecome, unmade, unconditioned. If, monks, there were not this unborn, unbecome, unmade, unconditioned, then there would be no escape from what is born, become, made, and conditioned. But because there is an unborn, unbecome, unmade, unconditioned, therefore an escape from what is born, become, made, and conditioned is discerned."' [1]

---

[1] This passage comes from the *Khuddaka Nikāya* in the *Sutta Piṭaka*, specifically from the *Udāna* collection. It is found in *Udāna 8.3*, known as the *Nibbāna Sutta*.

It emphasises Nibbāna (Nirvana) as the ultimate escape from the cycle of birth, becoming, and conditioned existence. The Buddha reassures the monks that because there is an unconditioned state (Nibbāna, Nirvana), liberation from suffering is possible.

Acknowledgement

I wish to thank James Whelan — a master of the English language and a seasoned dharma practitioner — for examining the manuscript, discovering potentially embarrassing errors both great and small, and making helpful suggestions.

Author's Note

Rebirth is a daring subject on which to write; some might say it is rather foolish to even try. All I can say is it is a subject I have found fascinating since my earliest introduction to Buddhism and which I shall, no doubt, continue to contemplate for the rest of my life.

Some Western Buddhists brush aside rebirth as a subject which can only be speculated on and so therefore not worth bothering with, but that is by no means a common perspective. What the Buddha did make clear was that it is pointless speculating on past or future lives. Seeing the nature of rebirth, on the other hand, is not speculative and is worth investigating, not only to discover what it is, but also to see the reality beyond it. As the Buddha said, 'The gates to the deathless are open!' Seeing the nature of rebirth, or birth and death, and awakening to the deathless, many would say, is the central point of the Buddha's teaching.

Though these few pages are a very brief outline of a vast subject, it is hoped they will at least stimulate an interest for further investigation.

Originally published under the title *Karma, Reincarnation and Rebirth* in 2002 by Thorsons, an imprint of HarperCollins, Publishers, this is a new revised edition.

Diana St Ruth

Preface

We know we are born, but not many of us remember coming into this world. We know we will die, but we don't know what will happen to us when we do. We know the name we were given at birth and what our nationality is, but we do not know who we are fundamentally, in the deepest sense.

We might have beliefs, even strong ones, about going to heaven or hell, or about being re-incarnated and coming back to live another life here in the world, or even being totally annihilated at death. Nevertheless, there are many of us who would have to admit that this life is a mystery into which we seem to have miraculously arrived and out of which we shall just as miraculously depart.

My spiritual journey began on my twelfth birthday when I saw something I didn't understand — my grandmother's dead body lying on her bed, cold and inert. I was stunned! perplexed!

What has happened to her? Yesterday she could hear the ticking of that grandfather clock — her body had life in it yesterday — but now her body is lying here unmoving like an empty shell. Her body is here, but where is she? Where is the person I know? I couldn't work it out!

It wasn't that we were close — my grandmother and I — or that she was a loving granny whom I was already beginning to miss. No, she was a formidable lady of the Victorian era — *Children should be seen and not heard!* — and I was frightened of her. Nevertheless, I wanted to know what had happened to her and what death was.

But no one seemed to know. Certainly the family members, by the way they were talking, didn't have a clue what was going on; but 'surely,' I thought, 'someone must have the answer! Someone must know.'

Not long after my grandmother's death, I asked a teacher at school what death was — which was out of character for me because I wasn't given to asking questions in class — but she turned away with some unconvincing remark, rather casually I thought. Nor did any of my rare attendances at church reveal anything, though I listened most carefully to every word the vicar uttered.

Some months after this I noticed my mother reading a book, and when I asked her what it was about, she looked at me rather thoughtfully for a moment and then hesitantly suggested I read it after her, which I did. And it turned out to be about something which I had never heard of at the time: age regression under hypnosis. The hypnotist delved into people's minds and got them to remember — not just to remember, in fact, but to relive — their childhoods and then back further to the time when they were born, and then back even further to *before* they were born. I was fascinated, and I wondered: *Can they really remember previous lives?*

I read the book from cover to cover, so fascinating did I find it, and then I was thirsty for more: *There must be more...* My mother didn't know, but she was as interested as I was. We both searched the bookshops, market stalls, and the library shelves for similar accounts. And this was when libraries came into their own for me. Books, I was soon to discover, are treasure troves of wonders, founts of information on fascinating subjects such as psychology, religion, the paranormal, philosophy, astral projection, — most outlandish topics, and mostly subjects I had never heard of before — but I found them incredibly wonderful, much more so than anything they were trying to teach me at school.

A lot of those books — compelling though they were — were way beyond my comprehension. Even so I tackled them gamely, undaunted — it was so exciting, and exciting to be on some sort of personal journey.

Over the following months and years I also came across the occasional book on Buddhism — there wasn't that much Buddhism available in those days, unlike the mountains that exist now — and it wasn't of greater interest than anything else I was reading, but gradually I became more and more drawn by it… there was just something about Buddhism…!

The Buddha was a man, just a person like me, just a human being who asked questions about life and death, searched diligently to find answers… and somehow found them! That impressed me greatly; that was something I could understand and it was what I wanted to do myself — I wanted answers to *my* questions about birth and death. So there came a time when I began to search specifically for books on Buddhism.

Finally, in the following years it dawned on me: *This is my path. I am a Buddhist.* The other topics — though still interesting — gradually faded into the background.

That original inquiry into death instigated by my grandmother's demise remained the driving force for me in those early years and to a great extent still do today. In fact, the inquiring kind of mind is encouraged in Buddhism; it is a way of keeping the doors open, of remaining free of dogma, of intellectual answers, and of egocentric conclusions about the profound nature of things. So, in Buddhism, deep life questions are regarded as a basis from which to work. They twist and turn in our minds, transforming and bringing insight into not only those particular questions but also into life in general.

A turning point in my search came many years later when I began to realise that questions about death and the mysteries of existence can never be answered in words or by the intellect, but rather felt, intuitively. And the questioning has to be centred upon one's own life. To ignore personal experience as though it were of no account would be alien to Buddhism which is an experiential journey into the mind. And its teachings are not just for the clever or gifted or those ordained into some religious order, but for everyone who feels inspired to look into this fascinating affair called 'life'.

The Buddha investigated form, feeling, sensation, mental activity and consciousness; in other words, he investigated the aggregates of himself and his own experiences as a human being. That approach of looking at what one is facing and experiencing is a distinguishing mark of Buddhism.

In the process, the Buddha observed cause and effect, action and reaction, becoming and re-becoming, the way conditions arise and fall away. And he put aside all of his beliefs, even the subtlest, while he was engaged in those investigations. He just looked at life openly without prejudice or judgement of any kind. As a result, he not only saw the existence of karma and rebirth, but also that which was beyond them.

It sounds simple and it is simple, though the simplest things in life most of us find the most difficult. It is certainly a subtle path, but the Buddha was determined and he got there. He saw that truth was not something fixed; he saw the spontaneity of it, the directness and totality of it — quite beyond words, and quite beyond concepts and ideas of any kind. This was the Buddha's experience and awakening, and it became the truth he expounded over the next forty-five years.

This book, then, is an investigation into what is born and what dies — the cause and effect process (karma and rebirth) — and also what is unborn and undying. It is therefore an investigation into impermanence, delusions which cloud the mind, and intuitive wisdom which frees it.

Introduction

It is worth making it clear from the very beginning what Buddhism is not: It is *not* a set of beliefs, a philosophy or a method of psychology, or at least it was never meant to be, though is sometimes used as such. It is rather a personal investigation into this life, into this very moment, which is to say into who and what we intrinsically are, each for ourselves.

Generally, in Buddhism, the encouragement particularly at the beginning of the search — is to question one's own beliefs and the nature of belief in general, and the effects belief and blind faith can have on our lives. It is often this kind of questioning that attracts westerners to Buddhism.

Of course, Buddhism is still a path; it is not a free-for-all where anything goes. There are those who seem to stretch and strain the edges of the teachings, in order to make them fit their own ideas, but generally speaking those who disagree with Buddhism's basic tenets will eventually go elsewhere for their spiritual nourishment.

The Buddha's teaching is therefore based on putting views, opinions and beliefs to one side and seeing things here and now as if for the very first time. It is an immediate way of 'knowing' without concepts and ideas. In other words, it is an opportunity to wake up from the dream of our beliefs and thoughts to something beyond thoughts. In Buddhism the word often used for this is 'enlightenment', though the word 'awakening' is probably more appropriate (the word 'Buddha' literally means 'awakened').

Chapter One

Hidden Beliefs

Rebirth and reincarnation are generally accepted realities in the East and have been since ancient times. *What* the next life will be is usually the question rather than *whether* it will be. In the West, on the other hand, we have our own religious and secular beliefs which usually do not include living another life, or at least not in this world or in this way. But unless one wakes up to the truth of it — East or West — one is still caught in cultural conditioning and personal beliefs.

It isn't difficult to recognise our heartfelt, clear-cut, major beliefs about heaven and hell, or reincarnation. Far more difficult to spot are those subtle beliefs; those hidden little things that lurk in the depths of our being, pretending to be facts. The sooner we spot those impostors the better.

One common belief, especially in our Western society which usually gets misidentified as fact, is that nothingness or annihilation is the actuality awaiting us at death. But this is just a belief! Can we ever experience nothingness? If we sit in a dark corner, cover our eyes, block up our ears and let our minds go blank, can we see nothing, hear nothing, taste nothing, smell nothing, and think nothing? Would that actually be the experience of nothingness? But who would be experiencing this nothingness? With what would nothingness be experienced? What is it actually that can ever know nothingness or annihilation?

It becomes clear when we investigate the matter, that, we cannot experience nothingness. To say we are experiencing nothing can only be a contradiction in terms. Ideas about nothingness preceding our lives and annihilation awaiting us at death are merely beliefs and ideas.

Philip Kapleau in his book *The Wheel of Death* put it this way:

'The assertion that nothing precedes birth or follows death is largely taken for granted in the West. But, however widely believed, it is still absurd from a Buddhist viewpoint. Such an assertion rests on the blind assumption — in its own way an act of faith — that life, of all things in the universe, operates in a vacuum. It asks us to believe that this one phenomenon, the invigoration of supposedly inert matter, springs out of nowhere and just as miraculously disappears without a trace. Most people who hold such views consider themselves "rational"...'

When we are free of all beliefs, including the belief in annihilation, then we are in a position to investigate *what is*.

Chapter Two

Karma

The Buddha referred to a natural law — the law of cause and effect *(karma)*; the principle that certain actions lead to certain reactions. Not all actions are karmic; not all actions lead to reactions; some are just life unfolding, but when we go against the way of things, as it were, the universe responds in kind.

Consider a stone thrown into a pond. The stone hits the surface and creates ripples. The ripples travel to the outer banks and on impact return to the centre, maybe pushing against the stone which caused them in the first place. This is a well known analogy of the cause and effect *(karmic)* process.

Karma comes into effect with particular motivations. When we crave or yearn for something, we usually go about trying to get it. That kind of craving is like the stone being thrown into the pond, and the actions which follow are like the ripples from that stone. These ripples have an impact on the world and there is a result. We cannot stop that impact and that return.

We are usually blind to the results of our thoughts, words and deeds. We don't always see the connection between what we have done and what comes to us maybe months or years later. Perhaps the person who is upsetting us right now is not the same person we upset in the past, but if we contemplate the situation, we might find that there is a distinct similarity between the two events, and now we know what that person went through on our account, so maybe we learn something from that!

In *The Light of Asia*, Sir Edwin Arnold's epic poem of the Buddha's life and teachings, 'a power divine' is referred to 'which moves to good'. And the poem proceeds:

> It knows not wrath nor pardon; utter-true
> Its measures mete, its faultless balance weighs;
> Times are as nought, tomorrow it will judge, Or
> after many days.

> By this the slayer's knife did stab himself; The
> unjust judge hath lost his own defender;

> The false tongue dooms its lie; the creeping thief
> And spoiler rob, to render.

The Buddha saw — and he wasn't the first — that we live out the consequences of our own deeds now or later. He had no doubts about that.

Ajahn Sumedho[2] put it this way: 'There *is* justice in the world. Even though you may not be discovered or punished by society, you don't get away with anything. You keep being reborn again and again until you resolve your karma. Here we are. How many lifetimes have we all had? We don't know, do we? But here we are. Here I am in this incarnation with my particular character and karmic tendencies.'

The thought that my own life was the outcome of previous existences had a profound effect on me when I first came across it: *This life of mine is the result of my own actions in the forgotten past? I'm not here by chance?* An overwhelming sense of joy swept over me. Suddenly I was not a helpless victim of mere chance or fate as I had previously thought. 'If the way I have lived in the past has brought me to this situation,' I reasoned, 'then the way I live now will affect my future.' It was an empowering realisation.

The Buddha likened karma to sowing seeds. 'The doer of good, will receive good,' he said, 'The doer of evil, will receive evil. Sown are the seeds and we shall taste the fruit thereof.' And he referred to freedom from conflict, anxiety and confusion within the mind as the finest fruit, the best and deepest happiness, rather than pleasure, wealth or any worldly success.

---

[2] An American-born Theravadan Buddhist monk.

First, however, we have to see that karma exists as a living reality in everyday life. As we become aware of the way our minds work and the resultant actions and reactions, we discover just how much anguish and suffering we create for ourselves and others; then karma becomes obvious and we do not have to take it on trust.

The first teaching the Buddha ever gave was about suffering. He said it is essential to acknowledge the suffering in our own lives, then to see its cause. If we look carefully, we shall realise that our suffering is caused, not by outer conditions or other people as we might have thought, but by our own states of mind, our own craving and yearning. 'The cause of suffering is desire,' said the Buddha.

When the cause is seen for what it is, we are in a position to do something about it. We can eliminate it, and once eliminated we find true happiness. In other words, the happiness of which the Buddha spoke is here all the while, but we cover it over with our own mind states. There is a path which the Buddha then referred to as the way of liberation from suffering. These truths regarding suffering, its cause, its cessation, and the path, are known as the Four Noble Truths, and are given great significance in Buddhism.

We probably already know deep down that craving for things we cannot have produces unhappiness, but most of us do it anyway, thinking that there is little we can do to avoid longing for what we want. But the more we catch ourselves wishing that we were slimmer, taller, smaller, younger, older, better looking, different, wishing we did not have to meet those people, or that the working day would end sooner, or that the boss would find another job, the more we realise that much of our suffering is something we bring upon ourselves.

It is hard, though, not craving for the things we want. And it is really only through seeing that craving and unhappiness are linked, that we are likely to do anything about it. First, however, we have to truly see that connection, get to the point of realising without doubt that negative motivations have negative results.

Chapter Three

Inner Suffering

Despair and anger might make us ask, 'Why did this happen to me? Why did I have to get caught in that accident? Why was I born like this? Why is it always my family that gets into trouble? Why can't I win the lottery?' We might feel we have been cheated, that life is cruel and unfair, and the temptation is to pin the blame on someone else: mother, father, husband, wife, partner, friend, society, the government, God. We think that if we were not in *this* particular situation, life would be okay, 'LIKE IT IS FOR EVERYONE ELSE!'

If conditions should happen to improve, however, are we happy then? If we get everything we need and more, have all our problems been solved? Maybe for a short time they will seem to have been, but then we have that sense of insecurity: *Okay, I've got what I want now, but what if I should lose it? What if it should all go wrong?* We cannot seem to enjoy some of our most pleasurable moments because we worry about what is going to happen in the future.

The truth is, of course, worldly pleasures cannot last forever and often don't seem to last very long. We might enjoy parties, but constant partying would become sickening and boring in the end... and we wouldn't mind if we never saw those lovely people again. The shiny new car may lose its lustre in the end; healthy though we are we may become ill in the end; we change our minds in the end; we die in the end...

That sense of uncertainty, that unease, that insecurity can follow us throughout life wherever we go, whatever the circumstances, spoiling everything, leaving us restless except for the most fleeting, fragile moments of an insecure happiness.

It is not surprising that we hate some of the things that come to us. We might find, however, that the greater suffering lies not in the situations themselves — terrible though they might be — but in wishing to rid ourselves of them and wishing for something better — not just once, but over and over again...

Anguishing about what we have or have not got, can often be a far greater suffering than physical pain. The anguishing might be related to physical pain — *we don't want it* — but the dread and despair we suffer are not themselves physical pain. We pile anguish on top of pain by longing for it to go. Desire first, then the impatience and anguishing... and then desire again, going round and round (cause and effect).

Bob was installing a lathe in an engineering factory some years ago and he got his hand caught between two parts. He managed to free it quickly, but felt this excruciating pain. Tucking the damaged hand beneath his armpit, he hopped around the workshop, moaning, groaning, cursing, pulling faces and generally making a great deal of noise and fuss. No one was surprised at the performance — *they would have done the same.*

During those antics, however, Bob suddenly realised that the pain was in the hand, only in the hand, and that there was no need to prance around pulling faces. And he thought: *I don't need to suffer; the hand can suffer on its own.*

He said, 'It was a revelation! One minute I was involved in pain, and the next there was *only* pain and somehow I wasn't involved in it!' He told me that this insight into the nature of pain was certainly the result of his Buddhist practice and that his perspective on life had completely changed as a result of it.

To allow the body to be painful when it needs to be, without regarding it as a bad thing, can be a liberating experience, a relief even, because there is no further conflict in the mind. Of course, it is difficult when pain is severe, but there is a way of separating oneself from it and changing one's relationship to it.

We reject pain and seek pleasure, all in the interest of happiness. Many people believe that pleasure itself *is* happiness, but if that were really the case, we would be happy every time the body experienced pleasure, which of course is not the way it is. Lonely, grieving people are not suddenly transported into states of bliss just because they munch on their favourite chocolate bar!

I like to eat; I like to sleep; I like to hear music and meet old friends, but when the phone rang one Monday evening to tell me my mother had died, I suddenly lost my appetite and my supper went cold.

Is it actually possible to rise above difficult conditions in life and not suffer from them? Or, is it possible, at least, to learn to tolerate them in a way which doesn't destroy our lives and make us downright grim?

I saw a leper sitting on the roadside once as I strolled by, chatting to a friend. I saw him and marvelled at his appreciation for the few rupees I slipped into his fingerless palms — *his smile!* Afterwards, my friend and I sat at a market stall drinking chai. Thoughts of that man with no ears, nose, fingers or toes, invaded my mind. He wasn't the first leper I had come across in India, but he made a deep impression on me. No human being could have had more to complain about, and yet he smiled that wonderful smile!

Chapter Four

Facing the Human Condition

Buddhist writer John Snelling had a terminal illness but he was able to demonstrate how it was possible to face fearful things and become enriched by them. He said, 'We all secretly think we're immortal, don't we, and that in our special case the gods won't give the fateful thumbs down. Yet at thirty-one I was having to face the fact that I was subject to sickness and death. There followed a period of great emotional turmoil for me. But one sunny morning I woke up to find I *could* accept it. I made this important discovery: human beings *can* face death with equanimity.'

John Snelling went one step further and came to the point of feeling that those years of illness were the richest and fullest of his life: 'Cancer and the knowledge of mortality threw things into perspective for me, showed me what the priorities were, helped me to grow and deepen as a human being. I also found my way to an authentic spiritual life.'

He said it saddened him to think that most of us tend to flee from the truth of our human condition, that we are all, without exception, subject to old age, sickness and death, 'What we need to rediscover,' he said, 'is that there's something ultimately unsatisfying about mere happiness. Yeats once observed that our lives really begin when we discover that human existence is basically tragic. It's only then that we get an inkling of its true grandeur and challenge, and appreciate the awesome duty we owe to our fellow human beings, our companions in this wonderfully strange and mysterious business.

'It is also true that only *in extremis* do we genuinely begin to uncover the spiritual dimension. In Christianity there's a saying, "Man's extremity is God's opportunity." So too, in Buddhism, a full appreciation of the fact of *dukkha* (unsatisfactoriness and suffering), is the beginning of the road that leads to wisdom.

'It's when the message hits us hard that we are only temporary sojourners in this world that we awaken to the fact that there's something larger and more magnificent than our petty selves at play here.' John Snelling lived for eighteen years with that cancer before he died, but he never tried to escape the truth of it or blame others. One should not get the impression he took on a loving persona as a result, however, or exude great compassion. On the contrary, he could be rather feisty at times, especially during his 'feeling well' periods. Nevertheless, he had a deep self-honesty and found a spiritual path that took him through the things he feared to something beyond.

Human beings *are* able to use difficult circumstances to spiritual advantage, uplifting not only themselves but also those around them. Sandy Burnfield discovered he had multiple sclerosis when he was a medical student. He didn't tell anyone and anguished in secret. Endlessly he questioned: *Why me? Why me? Why me?* His suffering reached the depths, but then after a very long time he said to himself, 'Why not me?'

His perspective changed and he suddenly saw the world differently. From that day on, his life was transformed. He still had the disease, of course, and still wished he had not, but then he saw himself as the bearer of something that people got sometimes rather than as a helpless victim of fate.

The circumstances did not change for Sandy Burnfield when his attitude changed, but the quality of his life altered in a remarkable way. No longer was his mind besieged by anger and despair, and he began to live fully again. He went on to become a consultant psychiatrist, following the course he had set for himself many years before.

Were those illnesses bad for John Snelling and Sandy Burnfield or good because of the transformations that took place in their hearts and minds? We all have our crosses to bare, shocks and disturbing events and things to cope with in life; we all have to face these things whoever we are. Are these difficult times bad? Or just the way life is?

In Buddhism one is encouraged to feel feelings fully, to know states of mind for what they are and to avoid attaching to or rejecting whatever comes along. One is encouraged to let things be, neither indulging in emotion nor prolonging grief. Nothing is to be brushed aside, nothing is to be regarded as too awful to contemplate or too stupid or too trivial to take notice of. Everything is to be acknowledged for what it is. This is a way of letting nature take its course and avoiding standing in the way of that natural flow.

We might feel that life has been unfair to us, that we have been picked out for unjust treatment, but we are all subject to the conditions of existence from the most heaven-like to the darkest of hells. If we are shaken by events, we can spiral into the depths of despair and have difficulty getting out from that pit of blackness. Or, if we take a step to one side and see beyond ourselves, distressing experiences can bring us into a new dimension.

Buddhism tells us — and we can see it for ourselves — that running away from unhappy circumstances is like trying to escape one's own shadow; it cannot be done. Only by facing things, by turning around and directly looking them in the eye, can we find a way through.

Sometimes we experience pleasure, at other times pain and discomfort even during a normal day; sitting in a comfortable armchair can bring aches and pains if we sit too long without changing our position. We might not like it, but there is nothing wrong with these things; it is just the human condition.

Chapter Five

Driven to Compassion

What happens if we are really put to the test? What if we are tortured, beaten, raped, shut in a prison cell for years on end, despised, starved? Surely, then we would hate life and not be so willing to accept the present moment for what it is.

I often wondered about that until I met a Tibetan Buddhist monk, Palden Gyatso, who had spent thirty-three years in prisons and labour camps undergoing the severest punishments and tortures. His 'crime' was that he had refused to denounce the Dalai Lama or to say that Tibet was a province of China.

During the 1959 Tibetan uprising this brave man led a peace march of about a hundred monks into Lhasa. He, along with others, was arrested. That was the beginning of a nightmare existence for him that was to continue until he finally escaped to India in 1992.

Until that time he was systematically imprisoned, released and imprisoned again with little time between to lick his wounds. He was just one of those troublesome characters the Chinese could not crush. Many died in similar circumstances, or committed suicide, or — unable to stand it any longer — succumbed to pressure and joined the oppressors. Indeed, many of those who tortured the political prisoners were themselves 're-educated' Tibetans.

Not long after his escape from Tibet, Palden Gyatso visited England and was asked to give a public talk in Devon. Beforehand some of us spent the day with him and he recounted his experiences:

'The pain I endured is beyond comprehension,' he said, 'I think the worst that can be done to a human being was done to me. There couldn't be anything more than that.'

'How were you able to deal with it?' someone asked.

'I survived — there was no magical formula. The pain came — I had no control over it — but I always had the absolute conviction that what I endured was somehow for the Tibetan people. I produced a sort of anger within myself to cope with it. Once I literally bit into my tongue and made it bleed whilst making a vow never to speak contrary to my beliefs. That was my determination.'

At sixty-four years of age he looked frail and a great deal older than his years. His back was bent, his arms crooked where they had been broken, and his teeth all knocked out from the electric shock of cattle prods being thrust into his mouth. Here was a man who had clearly been traumatised by those long years of terrible torture. Even so, there was an incredible gleam in his eyes.

'What were your feelings towards those torturing you? How did you feel about them?'

'Even though the punishments meted out to me were severe, I had no bad feelings towards those who inflicted them. They were doing what they were instructed to do by their superiors.'

'Is that how you felt at the time?'

'Yes, there were no feelings of revenge in me. If and when Tibet gets its independence, if we do to the Chinese what they have done to us, we would be as bad as them, if not worse. That was the kind of feelings I had when they were torturing me.'

'Did you ever lose faith in the Buddha's teachings?'

'On the contrary, my faith in Buddhism strengthened. The Buddha endured a lot of suffering throughout his lifetime. He endured physical pain and made many sacrifices for the benefit of other beings. Who am I next to him? My pain was no match for the pains of the Buddha. If I had died, it would not have been important. I could have died at any time, but I felt that my suffering somehow benefitted the Tibetan people in some small way.'

Palden Gyatso went on to talk about the meditations he secretly practised in prison. 'I meditated on karma,' he said, 'I realised that positive thinking and positive action paves the way to positive results, and that negative actions, physical or mental, go in the wrong direction.'

'Did you use any other particular practices to transcend the awful situations in which you found yourself?'

'Yes, I did. We can say prayers, but that's not it. The belief in pure honesty and justice are the basic tenets. One practises religion because one simply recognises the suffering of all sentient beings, great or small, and recognises that they are all seeking happiness.'

And, he repeated, 'I bear no grudge against the Chinese. If I did, I'd be going against what I believe. The Chinese are beings, we are all beings, and there is the recognition of their mistakes. That is religious feeling. Altruism is right motivation, a kind of determination to help other beings. When you have the wish to attain liberation for the sake of all beings, then you have a determination. This is not something vague; you have a conviction; you realise the necessity of helping others.

'Now, this torture went on and on,' he said, 'If I were to describe it in detail, it would be unbearable, and you might not be able to conceive or believe that one human being could do such things to another. So, not only would it be unprofitable to recall all the details, it would be very disturbing for me; it would provoke intense memories which sometimes produce a temporary anger in me. The memories also bring tears and make me cry, and they disturb my mind. It would also take a very long time to explain all that happened.'

Palden Gyatso was faced with great physical pain and deprivation, yet he came out of it with an incredible benevolence, compassion, and wisdom. At night, though, when he goes to sleep, he is sometimes back in those prisons being starved and tortured. And he suffers interminably at the thought of those left behind still struggling under similar awful conditions.

His has been a strange life, a life full of extremes, but it did not break him; the imprisonment and torture did not bring him down. He found a way of leaving the pain in the body, in the feelings, in the emotions, and rising above them all, knowing the difference between being positive in mind which brings positive results, and being negative which brings more suffering, even in those nightmare conditions.

Those of us who sat listening to Palden Gyatso that day agreed afterwards what a humbling experience it was. Before meeting someone like that one might doubt whether it is possible for a human being to undergo such horrors and remain sane afterwards, never mind coming out of it exuding the wisdom and compassion which came from him. It was deeply inspiring for all of us, and we couldn't believe our good fortune just to be in his presence.

Palden Gyatso knew about karma and followed its principles. It could be said that he was driven to wisdom and compassion. He could have gone towards bitterness, suicide, or compliance, but he chose something otherworldly and profound instead, transcending mind and body.

We all have these kinds of choices, although usually in less dramatic circumstances, and they can be times of opportunity. A much respected Thai monk, the late Buddhadasa Bhikkhu, used to say that suffering is both friend and enemy:

> It is only through unsatisfactoriness and suffering that we learn. We don't learn from being happy. We learn from mistakes and problems. Unsatisfactoriness is what causes us to grow in wisdom.

To whatever degree human consciousness has developed, it has only done so because of un-satisfactoriness. On the other hand, unsatis-factoriness and suffering bites, it slaps, it's painful, and it torments us. So suffering is also an enemy. And we're always trying to be free of it whether we realise it or not. We're always trying to run away and escape this enemy of ours. If we conceive both of these aspects of unsatisfactori-ness, however, as friend and enemy, then we shall begin to understand it on a profound level; we shall see unsatisfactoriness from the level of mindful-wisdom. This is knowledge that is based on awareness, self-awareness and an understanding of life. This is the opposite of stupidity.

If our understanding of unsatisfactoriness is foolish and childish, it will be of no use to us. By making use of what unsatisfactoriness offers us, we can develop the mind and grow in wisdom and understanding. By using unsatisfactoriness and suffering as a friend, there is less opportunity for it to become an enemy. Suffering and unsatisfactori-ness will then not bite, claw, scratch and torment us so much. This is a mindful and wise approach to suffering. Don't leave it on its own where it will remain an enemy![3]

---

[3] *Buddhism Now* magazine, Vol. VII, No.1, February 1995

Buddhadasa Bhikkhu advised his audience to make use of what unsatisfactoriness offers us. That, of course, is the basis of Buddhism: to take life as it comes and to see its nature.

Chapter Six

Siddhārtha's Awakening

The historical facts of the Buddha's life are debatable, though there is no doubt he lived and taught for several decades and went to the places he is said to have gone to. Nevertheless, as a legend — and there are several versions — it makes fascinating reading and at least helps to put the teachings into an historical context. But I think there is more to it than that.

For the most part in Buddhism, the teachings relate to oneself. Even the story of the Buddha's life, can be related to one's own experiences. The Buddha came to the truths he did as a result of deep sorrow. It wasn't that sorrow brought truth; it simply drove him to it. We might be able to relate to that!

His name was Siddhārtha Gautama and he was born approximately 500 BCE. His father was a nobleman, the ruler of a minor kingdom in Kapilavastu on the borders of present-day Nepal and India. But even though he was born into privileged circumstances, he suffered — not from the lack of anything money could buy — but from the plight of all beings, from the realisation that sickness, old age and death came to everyone. Right from childhood, therefore, Siddhārtha was more interested in the mysteries of existence than worldly pleasures. *What is life for? Are beings born just to die?* These were the types of questions which gripped him and which grew stronger as he grew older.

At the age of twenty-nine, therefore, Siddhārtha made a dramatic change in his life. He left family, friends and the comforts of his privileged existence in order to search for truth in more conducive surroundings and with others of like mind from whom he might learn.

Siddhārtha then spent the following six years wandering the northern regions of India practising all kinds of rituals and meditations, and sitting at the feet of those holy gurus he met along the way. He lived frugally, austerely, and experienced various levels of consciousness. But the teachings he learned did not satisfy him, and years of strict asceticism brought him near to death. So he began to take food again — at which point his five ascetic companions disgusted by his behaviour, took their leave of him — and he went on his way.

Siddhārtha was determined to continue his search for ultimate truth, and finding an agreeable spot, he sat in the shade of a tree, crossed his legs, straightened his back, and made a vow: *To come to truth here and now or never to rise from this spot again!* His determination was so great, so absolute, that he called upon the earth to bear witness by touching it with his hand.

Allowing anything and everything to come into consciousness without resistance, realising that he needed to see all states of mind and beyond them, he became like an open door watching what crossed the threshold but never going along with any of it.

First came the doubts: *Is it possible to realise ultimate truth? Am I being foolish to try? Is the bliss of concentration the best anyone can achieve? Maybe that is all there is to the holy life! Is life just a show? Am I not merely chasing the shadow of myself? Is it wise to sidestep those ancient rites and rituals?* But he recognised them all as nothing but a confusion of thoughts — and he let them go.

Then came an array of passions: lust, hate, greed, pride, self-righteousness and all the hopes, fears and emotions possible for any human being. He recognised them as false shows, and again let them go.

Eventually, memories and emotional states of mind passed, and then came the insights: he saw into the nature of time and timelessness, space and spacelessness, self and selflessness, suffering, the causes of suffering, and release from suffering.

And finally the supreme breakthrough came: Siddhārtha recognised, not only the re-becoming process, the truth of karma and rebirth, the truth of birth and death, but also that which lies beyond it: the unborn, the unoriginated, the unmade, deathlessness and the total freedom from all conditions. And he said:

Through many a birth I wandered in *samsara*[4], seeking but not finding the builder of the house. Sorrowful is it to be born again and again.

O house-builder! You are seen. You shall build no house again. All your rafters are broken. Your ridgepole is shattered.

My mind has realised the unconditioned. Achieved is the end of craving.[5]

What had shattered for Siddhārtha was the delusion of self, a self living in the world suffering this and that. No longer could the notion 'me' or 'mine' be taken seriously. His inner wisdom-eye had opened and he experienced a profound joy, a wonderful liberation from the darkness, turmoil and suffering of the deluded mind. Suffering and delusion, he discovered, went together as a pair, as do awakening and freedom from suffering.

---

[4] Samsara: The cycle of birth and death.
[5] *Dhammapada*, vv.153-154

Chapter Seven

The Buddha's Teaching

Now he was the Awakened One, the Buddha — no longer a person in the world, no longer Siddhārtha Gautama, the prince, the ascetic, the seeker. Realising that 'his own mind' was neither a specific, identifiable object nor a personal possession; he saw beyond form, feeling, perception, mental activity and consciousness; he saw beyond space and time, and he knew the end of suffering.

He realised an incredible awakening, an awakening into 'knowing', an illimitable 'knowing' which was not knowledge in the worldly sense but an intuitive wisdom. This was profound, deep, indescribable, inexpressible, beyond words.

So, then, how could he tell anyone about this? How could he explain it to his fellow sojourners, those who had been seeking as he had? It was as though he was mute, dump; he could not speak, he could not say anything about it and almost gave up any idea of doing so. But then an enormous compassion swelled up within him and he thought, 'Surely, there are those who will understand it, those with little dust in their eyes.'

So, he sought out his previous five ascetic companions and spoke to them of what he had realised.[6] He explained how to find the path of liberation from suffering, what to look out for and how to decide which way to go within oneself. The basis of his teaching for the rest of his life was that truth can only be recognised and cannot be passed on intellectually.

Perhaps the most succinct and well known example of this theme is given in a small text called 'The Kalama Sutta'.

The people of a town called Kesaputta, the Kalamas, had become concerned about the wandering mendicants who expounded their own doctrines and criticised others. The Kalamas increasingly became confused and approached the Buddha whose good reputation had preceded him. This is what the Buddha told them:

'Well might you doubt, well might you waver about a matter that is open to doubt. Do not be swayed by tradition, nor by scripture, nor by established principles. Do not believe a teaching just because you have heard it many times, nor

---

[6] 'The Four Noble Truths' — said to be the first teachings of the Buddha: To acknowledge the truth of suffering; to realise that the cause of suffering is desire; to recognise that the cessation of desire is the cessation of suffering; and to see the way to live in freedom from suffering (known as the 'Eightfold Path').

because you believe it to be true, nor because you have surmised or reasoned that it is true. Nor should you base the truth upon someone else's seeming ability or attainment, nor out of respect for that person because he or she is your teacher. When you know for yourselves that certain actions are unwise, then abandon them. When you know for yourselves that certain actions are wise, then cultivate them. See for yourselves whether greed, hatred and self-centred actions lead to misery. If they do, then abandon them. See for yourselves whether compassion and kindness lead to happiness for yourselves and for others. If they do, then practise them; do not abandon them. Base your way of life on them, and you will soon know the truth.'[7]

The Buddhist path is our own path, finding one's own wisdom right here, right now; it is learning to recognise the actuality of *what is* rather than spending time thinking about what others think and do, or wondering what we should do in the future.

---

[7] 'The Kalama Sutta', *The Gradual Sayings* (*Anguttara-Nikaya*), i.188

Chapter Eight

The Wheel of Life

The teachings of the Buddha have for centuries been depicted in all sorts of ways — as murals in caves and temples, as wall hangings, and as sculptures — and this has been a way of preserving and spreading those teachings. Not only are these often beautiful works of art, but they can also be more inspiring and more helpful than words.

The Tibetans have made their scroll paintings *(thangkas)* into a sophisticated art form. And 'The Wheel of Life' is a particularly well known and popular one — because, in effect, it is the story of our lives:

A great mythical creature (Yama, the Lord of Death) holds up a large disc. And this disc is a mirror, a circular mirror within which one sees reflected six realms of existence. These realms represent momentary states of mind, specific stages in life, or entire lifetimes. The point to realise is that these are realms we live in even in this life, irrespective of other possibilities that might exist.

The heavenly realm is generally depicted in the top section and the hell state in the bottom, with four other realms ranged between.

We know what it is like to be in heaven — if only for the briefest of moments — when everything is perfect, when everything is going our way, where we are overjoyed, intoxicated with success.

Another realm, 'the jealous gods', might also be familiar to us where we have enough for ourselves and yet crave what others have — their status, wealth, comforts, privileges. We are jealous of them and might even hate them for what they have.

Then there is the animal realm. Here, we are pre-occupied with our physical needs to the exclusion of anything else, just trying to survive in a harsh world — as victims perhaps, being servile to others — nothing more than our animal instincts occupying us.

And then there is the hell realm: torment, fear, despair, anguish, pain, untold suffering — most of us can relate to these things, at least sometimes in our lives.

And another rather special hell one might find oneself in is the realm of 'the hungry ghosts'. This is the torment of not getting what one craves or not getting enough of it — food, alcohol, drugs, power ... We get a little, we like it, we want more, but we can't get more. The desire grows and grows, becomes excruciating and we become consumed by it — so much so that we cannot function normally any more; and even if we get what we want, it never satisfies us; we have turned into ghost-like creatures — alive but not alive.

The sixth state on the wheel is the human realm. This is where our lives are more stable, on a more or less even keel, where our ups and downs are less stormy, where we are less troubled and less emotional. It is said that this is the easiest state from which to practise the Buddha's teachings, from which to see past one's delusions and to realise that all the realms are merely reflections of our own minds.

The Buddha is usually depicted in every one of the six realms, offering the truth, a way out, indicating that every state of existence from heaven to hell can be transcended no matter what.

At the hub of the Wheel of Life is a cockerel, a snake and a pig. They form a circle by each biting the tail of the other. These three represent greed, hatred and ignorance or delusion respectively — known as 'the three poisons' in Buddhism. They bite each other; they go together. And it is upon these three that the entire wheel depends; take one away and the axis collapses.

Around the rim of the wheel is a linked chain of events, which represents karma and rebirth, the cause and effect process — referred to as 'the twelve links of dependent origination'. There is no beginning or ending to this chain; it is a continuous round of: ignorance, impulses, consciousness, name and form, six sense objects, impressions, feelings, craving, grasping, becoming, birth, old age and death, one leading to the other. Our basic ignorance about what or who we really are keeps this process going. Death is the outcome of birth and birth is the outcome of death. Ignorance regarding the reality of life affects the way we live, and we continue going round and round in this vicious, relentless cycle.

When we are caught up in reacting uncontrollably to events, rather than acting from a position of clarity and freedom of mind, the links are locked firmly together, the process continues. If we rise above those conditioned reactions, the chain is broken and we are free of it.

So, the Lord of Death is holding up this great mirror and we can see the reflection of our own lives. When we see our lives in this way — as reflections — we become aware of conditions and yet are not caught by them. This is the function of the awakened mind, and the awakened mind is unborn and undying.

Zen Master Bankei once said that if we divide the day up into three parts, we would find that, of all our activities from morning to night, two-thirds are managed with the unborn. 'Yet,' he said, 'without realising this, you imagine you operate entirely through cleverness and discrimination — a serious error indeed!'

He continued, 'As for the remaining third, unable to abide in the Unborn, you change your Buddha [awakened] Mind for thoughts, attaching to things that come your way, so that even right in this life you are creating fighting demons, beasts, and hungry ghosts, and when your life comes to a close, you fall right into the Three Evil Realms.'

Bankei was referring to the lower realms on the Wheel of Life, but he rounded off his comments by saying, 'To believe the Three Evil Realms exist after you die is a great mistake, a bit of far-fetched speculation.'[8]

There are various interpretations of the Wheel of Life; it is for each of us to muse upon it and see what it means for us. Then, as an image, it can be very useful in our lives, just to contemplate its message.

---

[8] *Bankei Zen*, Peter Haskel

There are many aspects to life, many realms, many moments in the day, many states of mind. But whatever conditions prevail, there is always something beyond them. The moment can be full of suffering if we get caught in its conditions, if we take things personally, if we become a 'person' in the world, if we get caught in the cycle of events. On the other hand, we can go to something beyond.

Chapter Nine

Getting off the Wheel

So how do we get off the Wheel of Life, the wheel of karma and rebirth *(samsara[9])*? How do we come away from that round of hope and fear, joy and sorrow, pleasure and pain? How do we transcend the delusional world, the conditioned world, and find the un-conditioned, the awakened state and freedom from suffering *(nirvana[10])*?

Buddhadasa Bhikkhu[11] once said:

The Buddha taught that birth is perpetual suffering. What is meant here by the word 'birth'? In this context, the word 'birth' refers to the arising

---

[9] Samsara: Round of rebirth, the cycle of existences, lit. 'perpetual wandering' — the sea of life ever restlessly heaving up and down, the symbol of this continuous process of ever again and again being born, growing old, suffering, and dying. See also footnote 1, p.49.

[10] Nirvana, Skt., (Nibbana, Pali): Departure from the cycle of rebirths; absolute extinction of life-affirming will manifested as greed, hatred and delusion, and clinging to existence; the ultimate and absolute deliverance from all future rebirth, old age, disease and death, from all suffering and misery.

[11] Buddhadasa Bhikkhu (1906-1993), a Thai monk of the Theravada tradition.

of the mistaken idea of 'I', 'myself'. It does not refer to physical birth, as generally supposed. The mistaken assumption that this word 'birth' refers to physical birth is a major obstacle from comprehending the Buddha's teaching.

And he continued:

The expression 'freedom from birth' does not imply that one is not born again after physical death, that after having died and been placed in the coffin one is not reborn. . . If in the daily round there is only awareness, preventing the arising of 'I' and 'mine', the 'self'-idea, egoism — that is freedom from birth. When nothing remains but awareness, one is able to do what one has to do, and to do it properly. Under these conditions, doing one's job is enjoyable; to be able to do one's job properly without any 'I' or 'mine' is a joy. This is the essence of the Buddha's teaching. In effect it calls on us to live with a mind free from the idea 'I', 'mine'.[12]

We can see that 'I' is a word, a thought; it is born out of the conditioned mind and is just a way of thinking. We can see that, but we need to truly realise it before we will find freedom from birth and death. We are highly

---

[12] *Another Kind of Birth*, Buddhadasa Bhikkhu

conditioned beings and it is difficult to free ourselves of such old familiar beliefs and states of mind.

When we believe there is an essence, a soul, a spirit, an entity that somehow resides within the body or as the body — even as a subtle, shadowy one — then the 'I' is born; it is born in the mind and we live from it; but we shall live in fear of its death as well if we associate the mind and body with who we really are.

The Buddha referred to the word 'I' as merely a convenient designation:

> Just as that which we designate by the name of 'chariot' has no existence apart from axle, wheels, shaft, body, and so forth, or as the word 'house' is merely a convenient designation for various materials put together after a certain fashion so as to enclose a portion of space, and there is no separate house-entity in existence, in exactly the same way, that which we call a 'being' or an 'individual' or a 'person' or by the name 'I', is nothing but a changing combination... and has no real existence in itself.[13]

When we see change, we see birth and death, and yet we are *not* birth and death. To recognise that, is our liberation, our escape from death and birth, our escape from karma and rebirth and all forms of suffering.

---

[13] *The Word of the Buddha*, Nyanatiloka

Chapter Ten

Trying to See the Joke

Different ways of looking at things catch us at different times and that is why the Buddhist teachings are so diverse. It is not that we have to learn all the methods, study all the texts of all the schools, become engrossed in the history of Buddhism throughout the ages and learn all the languages the texts are written in, before we can get to the truth of it. Truth is not locked in a word or a description or even in a long stream of words. The truth is the same from first to last; it is about *us*; it is about what we are and what *is* beyond concepts and the thinking mind.

Descriptions are merely devices or skilful means for awakening, but they are not the reality itself; they are just hints: *Let's look at it this way; let's look at it that way. . .* They are all aids to help us open our own eyes. That is really as far as words and anybody's teachings can ever take us.

Trevor Leggett used to say that trying to point to the truth is a bit like telling a joke:

'Sometimes one sees a joke: it's enough. But if someone doesn't see it, or if it's an inappropriate joke, or if that person has no sense of humour, then it is no use labouring it — "You've got to see it!" — or arguing about it. Just pass on to another one.'

So too with all the descriptions, methods and techniques one hears about in Buddhism. If one doesn't get it, there is no point in labouring it; it is better to try something else. Somewhere along the line maybe one will catch us — like a good joke.

There is no point in plodding through mountains of texts and trying out every possible meditation technique. Once we find something that works for us we can use it; we can get to the very bottom of it, get on the path, on the right track and then keep going; no need to go back to the beginning again to learn another technique.

Whatever else, awareness is the key to the whole of the Buddha's teaching; it is the basis of all techniques yet is not itself a technique. There is nothing more obvious than awareness, but until we properly see what it is and realise its relevance, we might need various techniques to help us get there, like counting breaths while sitting in meditation, or naming each action we

take (silently to ourselves) throughout the day —
'walking', 'sitting', 'lying down', 'sneezing', 'eating',
'dressing', on and on — until one day we suddenly 'fall
in', we suddenly realise what awareness is, what being
at one with the moment is, its reality and its power. Then
the techniques are transcended.

Chapter Eleven

What Exactly is Awareness?

Awareness is something that does not come and go, so we don't have to create it or learn how to do it. It is here, innate within us, just waiting to be recognised

Being aware is a way of looking at life afresh without thoughts and memories; it is a way of experiencing each moment fully, seeing it just as it is. And when we make an effort to be aware, we merely make an effort to bring ourselves back into the present moment. It is in this context that the word 'awareness' is used in Buddhism.

One might also call it 'the inner eye', the 'eye of wisdom', or 'the Buddha eye'. We are trying to open this inner eye, this eye of the mind, so that we see not only conditions but also beyond them.

Insights will come as we practise. To begin with we just become more conscious of the material world manifesting before us. But gradually, if we are persistent enough, we shall begin to notice that awareness is not something that exists; it is formless, unborn, uncreated, unmade, unconditioned, neither a thought in the mind nor an object in the world. The more we realise this, the more we live by it and the more we experience freedom from conditions, freedom from birth and death; we experience, as Zen Master Bankei liked to say, the Unborn Buddha Mind:

'That which is Unborn is the Buddha Mind; the Buddha Mind is Unborn and marvellously illuminating, and, what's more, with this Unborn, everything is perfectly managed. The actual proof of this Unborn which perfectly manages everything is that, as you're all turned this way listening to me talk, if outside there's the cawing of crows, the chirping of sparrows or the rustling of the wind, even though you're not deliberately trying to hear each of these sounds, you recognise and distinguish each one. The voices of the crows and sparrows, the rustling of the wind — you hear them without making any mistake about them, and that's what's called hearing with the Unborn. In this way, all things are perfectly managed with the Unborn. This is the actual proof of the Unborn.' [14]

In this context awareness is unborn; it is our original

[14] *Bankei Zen*, Peter Haskel

nature because we do not have to look for it or create it; all we have to do is recognise it and use it. What needs to be avoided at all costs is taking on words like 'awareness' or 'unborn' — and imagining a nebulous, foggy voidness, thinking that that is it. That would merely be a product of the deluded mind, merely an illusion.

The ego-centred mind is very clever; it can protect itself by producing pseudo realities, and that is a way of avoiding the truth. This amazing feat of delusion is a real possibility and a real danger because we can start thinking we are enlightened. Unless we have enough self-honesty to recognise what we are doing, therefore, we could go completely off course without ever realising that this is delusion going about its normal business of blocking out genuine insight by getting caught up in rather grand ideas about oneself. The 'I' cannot be enlightened; the 'I' is a delusion. Enlightenment is what we are looking for, but becoming 'an enlightened person' is an oxymoron, an impossibility.

Chapter Twelve

I Want to Live!

If truth is truth, why isn't it obvious to everyone? Why isn't everyone enlightened?

In a way, of course, we *are* because the enlightened mind, the awake mind, is unborn, so it cannot be created or destroyed by anyone. As Bankei said, 'If we divide the day up into three parts, we would find that, of all our activities from morning to night, two-thirds are managed with the unborn.' [15] But if we are ignorant of this fact, then we are, after all, quite unenlightened; our eyes are coated with a thick layer of mental dust and defilement.

But, again, we could ask why is enlightenment not obvious when it is pointed out to us? Well, perhaps there is something in us that doesn't really want to know — in which case it doesn't matter what is pointed out to us we are not going to get it anyway.

Maybe we are afraid of letting go of our identity? Or

[15] See also Bankei quote p. 63

maybe we don't have any aspirations towards enlightenment because it sounds like a rather conceited pursuit?
In delusion, the ego comes up with a multitude of
excuses to stave off its own demise: *No, thank you. I
don't want to give up the self. I want to live, live!*
implying that if delusion falls away, we either completely disappear or settle down to very boring lives.

Ajahn Sumedho once gave an account of his own
experience along these lines:

'Before I started meditating, my world had a sense
of cohesion and stability to it, based on certain
limitations; and when those limitations started
falling away, it was very frightening: *The world is
falling apart! There is a sense of losing control!
I'm going to disappear into a void. If I don't have
this and I don't have that and I'm not like this and
that, then I don't know who I am any more; and I'm
just terrified!* That is an emotional reaction. But as
you trust more and see that that is just a reaction,
then it goes away. It is a natural reaction,
especially when you first start having those
insights.

'The Buddha, takes down all the barriers and
leaves an empty space. As you let go of your
emotional habits you find it is very peaceful, it is

universal, it is what you really are; you are not the limitations that you identify with. You are not the human body. What does that mean? If you think you are a human body, then the thought of the body being dead is rather frightening; your identities are limited to a physical body which is going to die. So then you begin to realise that your true nature is deathless rather than something that you are going to lose when the body goes.

'I remember in the early years of monastic life in Thailand — I was with Ajahn Chah[16] at a Thai monastery at that time — I found myself with this sense of dying; I felt I was dying and I got into this panic. I thought: *Luang Por Chah is trying to kill me. This whole monastic life is about trying to annihilate ourselves.* I began to fear I had joined some evil cult, and then I kept having these inner voices saying, "I WANT TO LIVE! I WANT TO LIVE!" and I was filled with incredible sexual desires; the most mad kind of lustful thoughts would come up in my consciousness, and this, "I WANT TO LIVE! I WANT TO LIVE!" But then I found that something in me intuitively knew not to act on it and so it began to fade out. . .

---

[16] Ajahn Chah, a Thai monk of the Theravada tradition (1917-1992)

'When I look back I see how frightening this sense of dying was. I used to contemplate Shakespeare's sonnet: . . .*and Death once dead, there's no more dying then*. . .[17] Luang Por Chah would say, "Die before you die!" He used that as a common reflection. In meditation therefore you might feel you are dying as a person — and that can be very frightening — but if you let everything die, what is left? It is deathless. So there is nothing to fear.'[18]

Buddhism tells us that 'self' is mind-built, thought-built, and that thoughts, views, and opinions deceive and distort. It also tells us that when the delusion of self dissolves, the reality becomes obvious. Reality doesn't disappear when delusion disappears, that would be a contradiction. Genuine awakening is not the end of what we are; all that ends is delusion — and that is no loss at all!

Ultimate reality is indestructible because it is not a thing. And even if delusions sweep us from fantasy to fantasy we are not those fantasies, we are not what thought invents or assumes.

The Buddha worked tirelessly throughout the greater part of his life to help others see what he himself saw. Just one look will reveal the truth, then life can be lived from it.

---

[17] Sonnet CXLVI
[18] From a talk given at the Leicester 2001 Buddhist Summer School.

'Since the light of a lamp can dissipate darkness that has been there for a thousand years,' said Hui Neng, 'so a ray of wisdom can do away with ignorance that has lasted for ages.'

Just a momentary recognition, they are telling us, will reveal the true nature of the mind, the true nature of what we are. And then we can go on from there.

Chapter Thirteen

Incalculable is the Beginning

As far as the so-called 'self' is concerned, not one single thing can be identified as being such a thing, yet life is being lived and experience keeps being experienced. That is the mystery! Life just *is* without our having to create it. Life does not need thoughts of a self for it to *be*; life does not need thoughts of any kind for it to *be*.

When we start to see that a self cannot be found in existence other than as a concept, fear might rise up within us: 'Where am I, then? Am I nothing?' It can be a terrifying sense of being lost. That is the mind going into protection mode because it cannot work things out.

We need to recognise that confusion comes from entanglements of thought and not from awareness. Putting one's attention on the here-now is not frightening. On the contrary, it is stimulating and strengthening, like waking up from a nightmare.

The Buddha realised that the essence of what we are, our true nature, never comes to birth. There is the born, but also the unborn — something birthless and death-less, something which has no characteristics, something which is not a thing. He saw that life is a changing procession of conditions, events, circumstances, a coming and going, a rising and falling without beginning or end, timeless and limitless. He said:

'Incalculable is the beginning of this faring on. The earliest point is not revealed of the running on, faring on, of beings cloaked in ignorance, tied to craving. . .

'. . .Which is greater: the flood of tears shed by you crying and weeping as you fare on, run on this long while, united as you have been with the undesirable, sundered as you have been from the desirable, or the waters of the four seas?. . .

'. . .For many a long day have you experienced the death of mother, of son, of daughter, the ruin of relatives, of wealth, the calamity of disease. Greater is the flood of tears shed by you crying and weeping over one and all of these, as you fare on, run on this many a long day, united with the undesirable, sundered from the desirable, than are the waters in the four seas.

'Why is that? Incalculable is the beginning of this

faring on. The earliest point is not revealed of the running on, the faring on of beings cloaked in ignorance, tied to craving. Thus, far enough is there for you to be repelled by all the things of this world, enough to lose all passion for them, enough to be delivered therefrom.' [19]

We try to own and possess life, command and manipulate it, make it into unlimited pleasure. The delusion is we think we can do it. The Buddha spoke about suffering endless births and the senselessness of doing so; he said that it was through ignorance that we put ourselves through it, and he encouraged us to abandon that way of life, to abandon the suffering we create for ourselves.

He spoke of 'this world' *(samsara)* which contains all negative states of mind, and another world *(nirvana)* that is free from negative states. He did not mean that there were two different worlds, two actual places — *samsara* and *nirvana* — but that our lives have two sides to them, like two sides of the same coin. He was pointing to the here and now, the vastness of this moment which has no beginning and no end, is timeless, and encompasses all that we are and all that we can imagine.

---

[19] Extract from 'Kindred Sayings on the Incalculable Beginning', The Book of the Kindred Sayings, Vol. II

The ending of rebirth, in Buddhism, is the ending of seeing 'self' as a separate entity, as some 'thing' that is born and dies. We can experience either *samsara* or *nirvana*, either the born or the unborn, and perhaps we can experience them both simultaneously, as one.

Chapter Fourteen

Taking Responsibility

It might be our habit to look to others for advice and guidance, particularly when it comes to issues we are in the dark about such as the true nature of existence. We look to religious leaders, holy texts, scientists and anyone in so-called authority. It might never occur to us to search within ourselves for answers to profound questions, and when we discover that the Buddha did exactly that and went on to suggest others follow suit, doubts might arise as to whether this is possible: *Surely we have to learn from others! Finding a great teacher and being guided by such a person would be the obvious thing to do, wouldn't it?*

The Buddha left his teachings behind, of course, so we *can* be guided by a great teacher if we want to be, but we might think it better to have a living, breathing teacher, someone we can ask personal questions of and who would be able to tell us what to do in our particular case; that would be nice, wouldn't it? But how would we find such a person? How would we find a wise teacher? How would we recognise anyone of that calibre even if we tripped over him or her? And if we were to find such a great being — or at least thought we had — what makes us think that that wise being would have the time or inclination to take us on and delve into the hidden recesses of our minds? The Buddha had transcended all notions of 'self', all desire for name and fame. He gave teachings and was available for questioning as he went from place to place, but in the modern context would he have advertised himself in a magazine or on the television, do you think? *Guru for hire!*

Not that we should dismiss help and guidance when it comes our way, but according to the Buddha, help and guidance are only valid if they direct us to the spontaneous wisdom within our own minds, otherwise we are merely taking other people's explanations of *their* insights which would only lead to pseudo insights.

The point is that even with the aid of good spiritual friends and wonderful scriptures, it is a journey no one can take on our behalf. It is *we* who use our own wisdom — we need to find and trust that — and with that wisdom it is we who decide what to practise, and it is *we* who put in the effort to do so, otherwise *we* shall never get insight into the nature of mind, into the nature of who *we* are!

The Buddha always warned about merely gathering information for its own sake without ever implementing it or putting it to the test. Acquiring information is not the same as seeing and knowing reality. As a living reality, truth can never be acquired, boxed and stored. The way is always spontaneous; we have to see what we see for ourselves — here and now — as it happens. It is no good simply believing what others tell us, going from one set of doctrines to another, from one belief to another, from one guru to another. The word 'Buddha' means 'awakened'. Siddhārtha Gautama became awakened by opening his mind to the reality of the present, the here-and-now, seeing and knowing for himself. And he made it clear that truth cannot be taught but only indicated, pointed to, hinted at.

The texts are mere maps; and teachers are mere guides. They have their value, great value if they are genuine, but they have their limitations as well; and we should be conscious of those limitations without feeling that having limitations is a flaw. They are limited in that they are guides only; we still have to 'do' it ourselves.

As the Buddha said:

Striving should be done by yourselves; the

Tathagatas[20] are only teachers. The meditative ones who enter the way are delivered from the bonds of Mara[21].[22]

Chan Master Hui Neng also said:

'The wisdom of the past, the present, and the future Buddhas, as well as the teachings of the twelve sections of the Canon, are immanent in our mind; but in case we fail to enlighten ourselves, we have to seek the guidance of the pious and learned ones. On the other hand, those who enlighten themselves need no extraneous help. It is wrong to insist upon the idea that, without the advice of the pious and learned, we cannot obtain liberation. Why? Because it is by our innate wisdom that we enlighten ourselves, and even the extraneous help and instructions of a pious and learned friend would be of no use if we were deluded by false doctrines and erroneous views. Should we introspect our mind with real *prajna* (wisdom), all erroneous views would be vanquished in a moment, and as soon as we know the Essence of Mind we arrive immediately at the Buddha stage.'[23]

---

[20] The Buddha referred to himself as 'the Tathagata' which means 'Thus come'.
[21] Often referred to as 'Mara the Evil One'; the personification of evil and the passions.
[22] *Dhammapada*, v.276
[23] *The Sutra of Hui Neng*, Wong Mou-Lam (trans.)

Treading the Buddhist path is seeing for ourselves what leads to wholesome results and following it, and seeing what does *not* lead to wholesome results and *not* following it. We can make those choices with our own in-built, innate, wisdom. We need to familiarise ourselves more with our own wisdom, or perhaps it would be better to say 'the wisdom accessible to us all'. If we are seriously intent on following the directions the Buddha gave, therefore, we shall tread the path and make the journey. If we only study and nod in agreement with things that sound logical, we shall miss the most exciting journey we could ever have.

Chapter Fifteen

Beliefs and Speculation

The Buddha, when questioned about his views on the mysteries of life, replied that he simply did not have any views and opinions.

Vacchagotta asked, 'Are you of the view that the world is eternal?'

'No,' said the Buddha, 'I am not of that view.'

'Are you of the view that the world is not eternal?'

'No, I'm not of that view.'

And Vacchagotta continued: 'Is the world finite or infinite? Is the life-principle and the body the same or is the life-principle one thing and the body another? Does the Tathagata [a designation of the Buddha] exist after dying or does he not exist after dying? Does the Tathagata both exist and not exist after dying? Does the Tathagata neither exist nor not exist after dying?'

In each case, the Buddha replied in what might seem to be the negative: *No, Vaccha, I am not of that view.* The

Buddha was refusing to offer views of any kind and he consistently said, 'Views are fetters which bring anguish and distress,' or, 'Views and opinions are not conducive to awakening.' These remarks of the Buddha were deeply profound statements about views and opinions themselves, the significance of which were apparently lost on Vacchagotta.

The Buddha was, therefore, not refusing to answer Vacchagotta's questions. Indeed, he was answering by saying, 'I don't have speculative views. By relinquishing all imaginings, all suppositions, the fundamental pride that "I am the doer," one is freed without clinging.'

Vacchagotta, however, didn't understand and asked further, 'But where does one arise whose mind is freed like that?'

'"Arise," Vaccha, doesn't apply.'

'Well then, does such a person not arise?' 'The term "does not arise" does not apply.'

And the Buddha continued responding to all of Vacchagotta's questions in the same vein. Finally, Vacchagotta gave up and said, 'I'm bewildered!'

'It's not surprising you're bewildered, Vaccha,' said the Buddha, 'this teaching is deep, difficult to understand and unattainable by mere reasoning. The

Buddha is freed from being denoted by material shape; he is immeasurable and unfathomable. "Arise" does not apply, nor does "does not arise", and so on.'[24]

The Buddha did not see himself as a thing crammed into a body, living bound by time and space, or as a being whom he thought of as 'me'. He made the point clear that reasoning would never get to the truth of it and that intellectual questions were useless, simply because they were intellectual, simply because they were limited to narrow forms of logic. But Vacchagotta didn't get it.

It can be fun speculating and wondering about life; we can let our imaginations fly. But if we really want to know something, speculating about it will get us nothing but frustration and confusion. And there is never an end to speculation; it just goes round and round; we just keep thinking and thinking.

Sir Edwin Arnold's wonderful poem, *The Light of Asia*, puts it like this:

Om, Amitaya! measure not with words
The immeasurable; nor sink the string of thought
Into the Fathomless. Who asks doth err,
Who answers, errs. Say nought!

---

[24] 'The Discourse to Vacchagotta on Fire', *The Middle Length Sayings* (Majjhima-Nikaya)

The books teach darkness was, at first of all,
And Brahm, sole meditating in that Night:
Look not for Brahm and the beginning there!
Nor him, nor any light.

Shall any gazer see with mortal eyes,
Or any searcher know by mortal mind;
Veil after veil will lift — but there must be
Veil upon veil behind.

In our spiritual journey, we shall come to understand that mortal eyes will never see the truth, nor the mortal mind know it. If you try to think this through, you will merely arrive at an intellectual conclusion through logic and reasoning.

Chapter Sixteen

Little Understanding

At one time, the Buddha was walking in a forest with his disciples. Picking up a handful of leaves, he said, 'The leaves in my hand are equivalent to what I'm saying to you, whereas what I *know* is like the leaves on the trees.' In other words, his own living experience was much greater than he was ever able to describe.

Again, this was not the Buddha suggesting that he was withholding information; it was rather his attempt at encouraging his disciples to become aware of truth for themselves so that they too could know 'to the extent of the leaves on the trees' instead of being content with 'the few that can be contained within one hand', a few scraps rather than full-blooded understanding.

Truth is not something one person can tell another — unless both parties are on the same wavelength and communicating intuitively, which in Zen is called 'transmission' — because the listener would merely be receiving a set of concepts and probably with the conceptual mind.

It is common for people on first hearing the Buddha's words to take the small things — the moments of peace, the initial insights — for ultimate realisation, not realising that they are just a small measure of understanding. This might be owing to a kind of arrogance on their part, thinking they have got there already, or it might be owing to a kind of laziness of mind: *This will do for me; can't be bothered to go any further!*

Buddhadasa Bhikkhu used to receive many visitors at his forest monastery in Thailand. He was well known and people from all over the world would flock to him. He suspected that some of them were just coming out of curiosity, so one day he said:

'An absolutely essential condition for the proper study of truth *(dhamma[25])* is the desire to be free of suffering and unsatisfactoriness. Without this intention to be free of all unsatisfactory mind states and dissatisfying conditions, we really won't know what we're doing and will just be muddling about.

'It's absolutely essential to have this wish to end suffering, otherwise the wish to meditate and study the teachings may just be the desire to follow a

[25] Dhamma, Pali, (Skt. dharma); phenomenon; object of mind; that which determines our true essence; the basis of morality; the teaching of the Buddha.

current fashion or a crowd wandering over from the beach!

'It's quite sad that most people seem to wander through life in a little cloud, as if nothing were wrong. And then, when something is obviously wrong, they pretend it isn't. People rarely develop the keen and powerful urge to be free of all forms of suffering, of all the problems and burdens that torment life.

'Without that kind of desire, we cannot practise. If someone threw you into the ocean and held your head under water for a couple of minutes, how great would your desire be to get out? The Buddha spoke of the feeling one would have if one's hair were on fire. If your hair were burning, if the flames were shooting up from your head, would you sit around twiddling your thumbs? Or would there be a desire to do something about it?

'Do you have the desire to extinguish unsatisfactoriness and suffering to the same extent that you would have if your hair were on fire? Is your desire that strong? Until you see suffering as central to what you do, what you say, what you think, you will never have the desire to understand it, to take it apart so that you know how to escape from it.' [26]

---

[26] *Buddhism Now*, Vol VII, No.1, February 1995

Buddhadasa was not being unkind when he said these things. On the contrary, he wanted people to get something genuine from Buddhism and from their visits to his monastery, something to radically change their lives — so he urged them on.

When the Buddha spoke of the way out of suffering, he did not mean it in a materialistic or limited sense — a person enjoying solitary, blissful states and avoiding disturbing or irritating conditions, or merrily whistling one's way through life with one's head in the clouds. Unless the illusion of 'myself' and 'my needs' is shattered, there will always be the tendency to go for personal satisfaction and physical pleasure above all else. Even living in a Buddhist monastery on one meal a day and strictly adhering to the many rules of the Order can be merely a chosen lifestyle rather than a genuine spiritual quest. The intention for ultimate realisation and freedom from suffering has to be present for the Buddha's teaching to be properly implemented. Otherwise we shall find ourselves being content 'with a small measure of understanding', or 'just muddling about'.

Chan Master Hui Hai said to his disciples one day:

'Once this poor monk [himself] heard the great Ma Tsu of Kiangsi say: "Your own treasure house contains absolutely everything you need. Use it freely instead of searching vainly for something outside yourself." From that day forward, I desisted.

'Making use of your own treasure house according to your needs — that can be called happiness! There is no single thing *(dharma[27])* which can be grasped or rejected. When you cease looking on things in their temporal aspect, and as having come or gone, then in the whole universe — above, below and round about — there will be no grain of anything which is not your own treasure. All you have to do is carefully contemplate your own mind; then the marvellous trinity of "three jewels in one substance[28]" will constantly manifest itself; of this there is no shadow of doubt.

'Do not search for the truth with your intellects. Do not search at all. The nature of the mind is intrinsically pure. Therefore it is written in the *Avatamsaka Sutra*: "All things have no beginning; and all things have no end." Before those who are able to interpret these words correctly the buddhas are ever present. Moreover, in the *Vimalakirti Sutra* it is written: "It is through your own bodies

---

[27] See footnote 25, p.98
[28] Buddha, Dharma and Sangha are commonly taken to mean the Buddha, the Doctrine and the Order of monks; to some they mean the Absolute, Universal Law, and the order of Bodhisattvas and Arahants; but to adepts like the Great Pearl [Hui Hai] they mean three aspects of one truth. (John Blofeld)

that reality is perceived; the Buddha is perceived in the same manner." If you do not follow sounds and sights so that they stir your minds, and if you do not pursue appearances so that they give rise to discriminations, you will then be unconcerned people.' [29]

The truth is there for the taking, no need to look beyond what we have, and no need to be content with a little understanding; it is a great treasure, not to be underestimated. This is the message throughout the ages of Buddhism.

---

[29] *Zen Teaching of Instantaneous Awakening*, Hui Hai, John Blofeld (trans.)

Chapter Seventeen

Rebirth-Reincarnation

The possibility of rebirth was news to me when I first heard about it many years ago, but the idea instantly gripped me. The thought that life stretched into infinity seemed to open all the windows and doors in my confined world.

What I did not realise in those early years was that there was an enormous difference between the word 'rebirth' (generally used in Buddhism) and the word 'reincarnation' (used elsewhere); to me they were synonymous. It was not until I began to look more carefully at what the Buddha meant by 'the delusion of self' that I started to differentiate these two terms in my own mind.

'Reincarnation' implies the existence of an entity, a self, a soul or a spirit which exists within the physical body and then, when the time comes, moves on to occupy the body of an unborn child — re-incarnating and living again as another person in another life.

The Buddha's teaching of rebirth or the rebecoming process, on the other hand, is about constant change and the transformation of conditioned phenomena, the constant flow of form, feeling, perception and mental activity — all moving and transforming from moment to moment, tirelessly, endlessly. And within that process no identifiable, unchanging soul, spirit, divine spark, or 'self' of any kind can be found.

The Buddha saw beyond the impermanence of conditions something most of us do not see. He became aware of an unconditioned, an unborn, an uncreated, an unmade. He saw conditioned phenomena — which we might mistake as 'self', 'myself', 'me' — but also the unconditioned which cannot be identified as anything whatsoever, but which functions, which sees with the mind, which knows.

Again, this is not a concept to get our heads around, learn and remember. If we treat it as such we shall never experience it; it will merely be a meaningless bit of information that we remember sometimes, forget sometimes and get confused about sometimes.

Zen master Shunryu Suzuki roshi once said:

'After some years we will die. If we just think that it is the end of our life, this will be the wrong understanding. But, on the other hand, if we think that we do not die, this is also wrong. We die, and we do not die. This is the right understanding. Some people may say that our mind or soul exists forever, and it is only our physical body that dies. But this is not exactly right, because both mind and body have their end. But at the same time it is also true that they exist eternally. And even though we say mind and body, they are actually two sides of one coin.'[30]

Although, in general, Buddhism refers to rebirth and not reincarnation, in the Tibetan form of Buddhism the word 'reincarnation' is often used. It is said that accomplished practitioners are able to intentionally reincarnate at the end of their lives in order to continue their dharma (spiritual) work, and these reincarnated practitioners are called *tulkus*.

The present Fourteenth Dalai Lama is a case in point. He is regarded as the reincarnation of the previous Thirteenth and all the other Dalai Lamas before him. All these individuals are believed to be linked from life to life, almost like one continuous life over the centuries. When asked about this, the Dalai Lama hesitated rather, but then said that when he was a boy he learned certain things very quickly and it felt like the rekindling of old memories rather than the learning of new things.

Despite references to reincarnation, however, and the

---

[30] *Zen Mind, Beginner's Mind*, Shunryu Suzuki

tulku phenomenon, Tibetan Buddhism retains the basic teaching of rebirth as taught in other forms of Buddhism. It isn't that Buddhists in general think that life does not continue after the death of the physical body, or that one does not again take birth as a human being after this life, but that 'self' is not an object which exists in the first place. The Buddha taught that there is no unchanging nugget of a being which continues from one moment to the next, or one life to the next throughout eternity. Not only the 'self' but 'time' is a delusion — that is what Buddhism points out.

The Tibetan understanding of reincarnation, therefore, does not involve the notion of a fixed self-entity or a fixed anything, and during the debating sessions a common question might be: *If the self is a delusion, what is it that reincarnates?* So they try to avoid falling into the trap of either the nihilist or the eternalist point of view. The young monks in training tussle with conundrums like this. It becomes a sort of challenge to try and catch each other out, and they have some fun with it. It is certainly a way of getting to know the teachings inside out, and hopefully to gain real insight into them so that the answers are not merely learned parrot-fashion.

Seeing into the essential nature of 'self' is therefore central in the practice of Tibetan Buddhism as with all other forms of Buddhism.

What we really are is not born at all! This is what the Buddha taught. And this, when realised, is a great liberating experience which invalidates such questions as: *Shall I be again?*

Chapter Eighteen

Beyond Words

All concepts are mind-constructions; they are based on speculation and some kind of logic, but they are not real knowledge in the sense of immediate 'knowing'. We cannot really know anything by concepts because what we genuinely know is quite spontaneous and basically indescribable.

Buddhism emphasises that we are the *only* ones who can know what is going on for us. Absolute truth is the truth of what we *know* without the concepts and explanations; it is about ordinary experience, real experience beyond words.

Seung Sahn[31] was fond of talking about the 'don't know mind'. He impressed on his audience the importance of this 'don't know'. This is not a fuzzy 'don't know', a 'hope to know in the future', or a hazy or dull state. Not knowing in that sense is only the intellect not knowing. There is another kind of 'don't know' that

---

[31] A Korean Son (Zen) monk (1927-2004)

arises from an intelligent, insightful clarity, and that is quite different.

Addressing an audience once, Seung Sahn said, 'Life is like the appearance of a floating cloud, and death is like the disappearance of a floating cloud. The floating cloud does not exist. A human being coming and going, birth and death, are also like that. Our body is like the floating cloud. But there is one thing that always remains clear which is not dependent on birth and death.

'What is the one pure and clear thing? If you find it, you will have freedom from birth and death. So, where do you come from? Don't know, right? I ask you, what is your name?'

[Someone in the audience responds with his name.]

'That's your body name,' said Seung Sahn, 'not your true self name.

'How old are you? Maybe you understand body age, but you don't understand true age.

'When you die, where do you go? Don't know, right?

'So, coming — "don't know"; name — "don't know"; age — "don't know"; going — "don't know". You *are* "don't know". That is "don't know mind".'

Seung Sahn also related the words of a famous Zen master who would say: 'Understand your true self'. One day, one of that master's students asked, 'Do you understand *your* true self?' The master responded, 'I don't know, but I *understand* this "don't know"!'

'That is a famous "don't know" classic,' said Seung Sahn. 'So, this "don't know" mind is very important.'[32]

What is happening in this moment is reality — we can be aware of it, we can know it, but we can only really know it as Seung Sahn said with the 'don't know' mind, with the non-conceptual, intuitive mind. Once we place a name on the spontaneous uprising of life, once we describe it to ourselves and file it away for future reference, that description is likely to stand in our way and the living reality be distorted.

The Taoists say:

The Tao [the Way of things] that can be told is not the eternal Tao. The name that can be named is not the eternal name.[33]

Likewise in Buddhism, reality is seen to be neither an object nor a subject, but just the experience itself, the *knowing* experience. If we attempt to capture absolute reality in words and descriptions, we might think we are understanding it, but we are merely making do with echoes and distortions.

In experiential terms, 'mind' is but a word, 'self', 'time', 'place', 'past', 'present' and 'future' are all just

---

[32] *Cutting Edge*, Vol.1, No.1, 1985
[33] *Tao Te Ching*, Lao Tsu, Gia-Fu Feng and Jane English (trans.)

words. They have symbolic meaning and they allow us to communicate with others on a conventional level, but that is all; they are not the full story.

We might believe that the mind is like a small powerhouse located in the brain behind the eyes encased in a skull. Some brain surgeons might also believe that, but they cannot actually pinpoint it and say: 'There! That's the mind.' The word 'mind' is a rather nebulous term which we often just regard as an immaterial part of ourselves.

If we take the Buddha's advice and begin to seriously look at what we experience, we might discover that what we call 'mind' is neither identifiable nor locatable! It is rather intangible, limitless, mysterious, impossible to fathom and define.

When we set out to discover the true nature of existence and the true nature of what we are, we attempt to look directly, to become clearly aware of what we feel, what we see, what we hear, what we taste and what we know *without* the concepts, *without* the judgements, *without* the mental proliferations; we attempt to get under the skin of experience and resist that veil of thought which, in the beginning, at least, threatens to fall over our eyes at any given moment and obscure our vision once more.

It is not that thought is a bad thing — it is a natural

function and a useful one like seeing and hearing — but we tend to think too much, dream too much, plan too much, and give it too much credence, allowing ourselves to be fooled by it. We trust thoughts, views and opinions sometimes more than we trust the direct impact of the reality in front of us.

Chapter Nineteen

Intuitive Wisdom

There is something within us which knows exactly what is going on at any given moment without words, without thoughts, without ideas, concepts or beliefs; and it is entirely spontaneous and awake. This we can call 'awareness' or 'knowing' but occasionally it can be such a striking moment of insight that we might give it greater significance by referring to it as 'intuition' — 'intuitive understanding' or 'intuitive wisdom'.

Many people experience these extraordinary moments of intuition from time to time, but very often they are so fleeting, they go virtually unnoticed — *just a vague sense of something that crosses the mind and then... gone!* So it gets brushed aside and forgotten. On other occasions it can be so obvious that we really cannot ignore it and probably never forget it for the rest of our lives.

When I was about eight years old I was walking home from school one day. I was on my own — *I had been instructed to walk with friends!* — and for some reason I started paying close attention to the traffic on the busy road along which I was wending my way. The wheels of the buses and lorries were so big to me, and it was as if I became mesmerised by them. And then I found myself somehow wondering what it would be like to be run over. For a moment or two there was quite a strong impulse to actually do it. It didn't feel like a suicidal moment; it was just that I wanted to know what it would be like to be dead. And then two things came to me in quick succession: Firstly, that my mother would be very upset if I got killed; and secondly — and this I would now call 'intuitive' — was that 'nothing would happen'. I somehow knew, and I questioned it no further because it was such a strong feeling, that being dead was no different from being alive. And it was a very matter-of-fact kind of knowledge, though I have never forgotten it.

These occasions of intuition do not have to be related to anything spiritual or extraordinary, however, they might just be things that happen to us in normal daily round.

Jacob worked for a supplier of food equipment. One day the company took delivery of a machine which, upon inspection, was found to have a strange fault; it turned itself off and on in quick succession without a break. This was a problem the site engineer had to attend to, but he had never come across such a thing before, and it completely baffled him. He checked the contacts, solenoids and wiring, but for the life of him, he could find nothing wrong with that machine, and left work that evening scratching his head.

The following day Jacob, a field engineer, was called in from his normal work to see if he could do any better. Going over the same ground, he ended up in the same place — completely nonplussed.

On his way home, Jacob thought of nothing else except that machine, and climbing into bed that night the dilemma rumbled on, gnawing away at him. Finally, he started to drift off to sleep — his thoughts gradually slipping away. But then, in that state of being neither awake nor asleep, he had the vision of the wiring diagram of that machine. In that moment, in that state of half-sleep, he saw with his mind's eye, where the fault lay: A wire had been placed on the wrong side of one of the solenoids.

The following day Jacob went to work and followed through on the vision that had come to him the previous night, and — hey presto! — the machine worked perfectly.

Jacob maintained that he could never have worked out logically what was wrong with that machine, and he was convinced that the only reason he discovered the fault was because he had experienced something which could only be described as a vision or a moment of intuition.

The cynic in us might come up with all kinds of rational answers to dispute such a possibility, but people who experience occasions like these know the difference between an instant realisation of something and normal reasoning or thinking.

Going back a few centuries to the ninth-century, there was a Chan (Zen) monk by the name of Hsiang-yen. His knowledge of the texts was extensive. One day his teacher asked him — *and this was a typical Chan or Zen type of question* — 'What was your original face before your parents were born?'

Hsiang-yen couldn't give an immediate answer, so he contemplated it. But, though he tried very hard, he couldn't find the answer, even though he searched through the books — his fount of knowledge — but to no avail. Finally, in desperation, he asked his teacher what the answer was. But the teacher refused, saying that passing on mere words was useless.

Greatly disappointed and in a state of dejection Hsiang-yen burned his precious books and left the monastery with the words: 'The picture of food cannot satisfy an empty stomach.' The realisation that none of his learning and erudition was of any use to him when he needed it; it was a bitter blow.

Some time later Hsiang-yen came across an old grave that needed tending. Having nothing better to do he settled into the nearby hermitage and began caring for the grave. He could not, however, forget his teacher's question which continued to play on his mind: *What was your original face before your parents were born?*

One day, whilst sweeping around the grave, a pebble flew up from his broom and hit the trunk of a bamboo tree. The sharp sound of the pebble against the bamboo struck through his stream of thoughts, and as it did so Hsiang-yen had a sudden awakening. It was a deep, indescribably sublime realisation that brought great joy.

He immediately burned incense to his teacher in gratitude, for the first time realising the purpose behind such a question — *What was your original face before your parents were born?* — and why his teacher had refused to tell him the answer 'in mere words', words which might temporarily satisfy the intellect but which would cheat him of the awakening he had.

Having gone through the usual process of trying to answer a question with the worldly mind, Hsiang-yen finally saw the vast difference between intellectual knowledge (he had been very attached to his books), and intuitive wisdom.

When Jacob, the engineer, stopped trying to logically work out what was wrong with that faulty machine and began to drift off to sleep; and when the Buddhist monk, Hsiang-yen, gave up trying to think of the answer to that seemingly illogical Chan Koan *(kungan)* given to him by his master, another part of their minds became active. In both instances, suddenly, the answers appeared; there arose dramatically as if from nowhere, vividly, spontaneously, bright and clear. As one well-known Buddhist analogy goes:

> 'The sun shines always, but when the clouds block it out, it cannot be seen. It may seem that the sun isn't shining any more, but once the clouds disperse, it shines brightly again.'

Once our emotions and proliferating thoughts settle, once our minds cease to struggle and instead become fully aware of this moment, the unborn, the awakened buddha-mind shines forth as it always has done since beginningless time.

Chapter Twenty

Life is a Koan

In China and later in Korea and Japan a unique method of practice developed using something called 'the *koan*' (Jap.)[34] — a type of conundrum which can never be solved intellectually. Intellectual questions are to be answered with the intellect — and that is the way it should be — but Chan or Zen questions are meant to draw on the intuition, to generally expose the intuitive mind to the practitioner, and bring forward the experience of insight.

There are classical koans — those that have been recorded and used time and again over the centuries — and there are natural koans — those that emerge unbidden from the depths of one's being.

Examples of classical koans are:

- *Give me the essential word about your self before you were born, before you knew either east or west.*

---

[34] *kung-an* (Chin.)

- *In clapping both hands together a sound is heard. What is the sound of one hand?*

- *Why is it that a man of great strength cannot lift his leg?*

- *What is this?*

In a monastic or retreat situation where a koan is given by the master, the student is required to work on such a koan continuously, day and night, whilst sitting in formal meditation, and whilst going about one's everyday activities. And if the koan is diligently and continuously contemplated — which is the kind of determination required in this type of practice — it will not be forgotten even during sleep. When the koan practice gets to this level, it becomes the most predominant feature in one's life and will begin to work on every stratum of consciousness, no matter what other activity one is engaged in. By this means, the ground is prepared for a breakthrough into the clarity of the awakened mind.

When first taking on a koan, most people treat it in the way they treat any dilemma in life — by applying reason and logic. But the koan will never relinquish its secrets to reason and logic. One has to take a step beyond those lines of thought and mental proliferations for a realisation to arise.

Soko Morinaga, a Japanese Zen roshi, visited Britain during the 1980s and 1990s to lead retreats at the invitation of the Buddhist Society, London. Usually about a hundred people participated in those retreats which meant that the roshi did not have enough time to give individual interviews, and so the interviews were dispensed with. An air of disappointment suffused the atmosphere when this was announced: *After all, this was the big opportunity to face a genuine Zen master from Japan on a one-to-one basis; something most of us had only read about and were looking forward to.*

People slouched from the hall rather dejectedly that evening, grumbling under their breath, but Trevor Leggett — himself an accomplished Zen practitioner and teacher — said loudly enough for us all to hear: 'Highly overrated!' as he swept from the room.

It was clear what he meant: Personal interviews with Zen masters are not *that* important. What *is* important — and deep down probably everyone knows it — is to practise seriously and to let the practice itself carry one through, without depending on one-to-one interviews with teachers. Not even great Zen masters, after all, can take us by the hand and lead us to awakening. It is good to have genuine spiritual friends, there is no question about that, but basically we are on our own.

As it happened, it *was* possible to speak personally with this powerful Zen man on those retreats. It wasn't the formal set-up one would find in Zen monasteries; it was over afternoon tea in a relaxed atmosphere, and under the circumstances far more befitting the occasion. People were able to speak freely, and something profound and precious came from those moments of interaction.

It was during one of those sessions that a member of the group, Richard, related to the Roshi how he had struggled with the famous koan: 'Nansen Kills the Cat'.[35] Richard loved animals and particularly cats which is why this particular koan had held his attention for so long. He said that he could not believe that the koan really had anything to do with killing a cat!

The Roshi said, 'You should carry on with that koan, it's got under your skin.'

Richard did carry on with it and on the following year's retreat during a similar afternoon session the Roshi, quite unexpectedly, turned to him and asked,

---

[35] Once the monks of the Eastern Hall and the Western Hall were disputing about a cat. Nansen, holding up the cat, said, 'monks, if you can say a word of Zen, I will spare the cat. If you cannot, I will kill it!' No monk could answer. Nansen finally killed the cat. In the evening, when Joshu came back, Nansen told him of the incident. Joshu took off his sandal, put it on his head, and walked off. Nansen said, 'If you had been there, I could have saved the cat!'

[*Zen Comments on the Mumonkan*, Zenkei Shibayama]

'How are you getting on with "Nansen Kills the Cat"? (Out of a hundred participants, it was impressive that the Roshi had remembered this particular person and also his interest in this particular koan.)

In reply, Richard said: 'Still struggling.'

The Roshi rose to his feet, walked over to Richard — getting so close that their noses were mere inches apart — and yelled in English (which was also surprising since he usually spoke through an interpreter): 'YOU ARE THE CAT! YOU ARE THE CAT!'

The room went deadly quiet and Richard looked stunned, as did everyone else.

Later Richard related how earth-shattering that moment was for him. 'At the moment the Roshi shouted in my face,' he said, 'there was a kind of dropping away of 'self', my very being...!', but he couldn't really describe it.

Whatever had happened to Richard on that occasion, it clearly had a profound effect on him, and also on those who witnessed it. It was some kind of spiritual gift.

Not everyone has the opportunity to meet outstanding people like that roshi. It is marvellous if it happens and even more wonderful to have personal guidance from such a person, but it is not a prerequisite to awakening.

Soko Roshi once talked about personal koans — those which arise naturally from deep within oneself —

as distinct from the classical ones presented by a master or chosen from a book.

He made the point that life-dilemmas should not be ignored or regarded as inferior to the classical koans, as they can work just as well, if not better.

When something starts to gnaw away at us to the extent that we can think of nothing else, that could be a koan with which we could work. It might be anything: A difficult relationship, a great loss, a hurt or injustice, illness — anything that makes us ask: *Why? Why? Why? Or it could just be life itself suddenly seeming to be a complete puzzle! The universe — What is it? Birth, ageing and death — What are they? Why am I? What am I?*

The Buddha found genuine truth within himself and, as he later said, so can anyone who wants to. The real Zen Master lies deep within ourselves; not within those superficial ego-centred delusions, but in the wisdom and compassion that is accessible to us because it *is* us.

It is a great boon to have the personal guidance of a genuine Buddhist master, but equally it might not be our karma for that particular eventuality to arise in our lives. Very few people have a formal Buddhist training, and even if they do, they might not be ready to benefit from it. Whatever happens, eventually we have to turn the spiritual eye upon ourselves. We don't need anyone else or any special circumstances to do that.

If we feel there are mistakes in the universe or that we have been unlucky, and if we then carry a grudge around with us because of it, we shall never find our way out of the karmic cycle. There will always be something wrong. We shall always feel like helpless victims without a chance... until it is just too late (for this life at least).

Whatever technique one might adopt in Buddhism, the most important thing to bear in mind is that every single one of them has to be transcended in the end. They are all just aids, devices to help us on the way, help us come to awareness, just simple awareness which is here all the while, which is no technique at all.

Chapter Twenty-one

Catching on

Zen Master Bukko[36] said:

'The way out of life and death is not some special technique; the essential thing is to penetrate to the root of life and death. It is in the centre of everyone, and everything else is dependent on it. Zen is to pierce through to it.

'Zen sitting is not some sort of operation to be performed. It is going into one's true original nature before father or mother were born. The self seeks to grasp the self, but it is already the self, so why should it go to grasp the self? Look into it. Where was it then? Where is it now? When life ends, where does it go? When you feel you cannot look any more, look and see how that inability to look appears and disappears.

---

[36] Bukko (Buddha-Light) was an honorific title bestowed posthumously by the Japanese Emperor on a Chinese monk, Tsu Yuen, one of the thirteenth-century Buddhist teachers who took Zen to Japan.

'As you look and see how the looking arises and goes, *satori* (realisation) will arise of itself.

'At the beginning you might take up a koan riddle. One such is: W*hat is your true face before father and mother were born.* For one facing the turbulence of life and death, such a koan clears away the sandy soil and opens up the golden treasure which was there from the beginning, the ageless root of all things.

'In concentration on a koan, there is a time of rousing the spirit of inquiry, a time of breaking clinging attachments, a time of furious dashing forward, and a time of damping the fuel and stopping the boiling. In general, meditation has to be done with urgency, but if after three or four years the urgency is still maintained by force, the tension becomes a wrong one and is a serious condition. Many lose heart and give up. In such a case, the koan is to be put down. Then there is a cooling. After a time, the rush of thoughts outwards and inwards subside naturally, and the true face shows itself as the solution to the koan. And mind, free from all motivations, always appears as void and absolute sameness, shining like the brightness of heaven, at the centre of the vast expanse of phenomenal things, and needing no polishing or cleaning. This is beyond all concepts, beyond being and nonbeing.

'Leave your innumerable knowings and seeings and understandings, and go to that greatness of space. When you come to that vastness, there is no speck of Buddhism in your heart, and then you will have the true sight of the buddhas and patriarchs. The true nature is like the immensity of space, which contains all things. When you conform to high and low, square and round, to all regions equally, that is it. The emptiness of the sea lets waves rise, the emptiness of the mountain valley makes the voice echo, and the emptiness of the heart makes the Buddha. When you empty the heart, things appear as in a mirror, shining there without differences in them: *Life and death is an illusion, and all the buddhas one's own body.'* [37]

We might never take on a koan as a practice — it can be difficult without a good teacher to guide us — but other techniques work just as well. To know the principle behind the koan practice can be of enormous help in understanding how intellect can block intuition.

Some time during the thirteenth century, a Japanese

[37] *The Old Zen Master: Inspirations for Awakening*, Trevor Leggett

Pure Land Master, Ippen, was watching some children playing with a spinning top. The top fell to the ground and lay there. This triggered a great insight in Ippen which he later recounted:

'Going over this in my mind, I saw that if you spin a top, it will turn, and if you do not go about spinning it, it will not turn. Our turning in transmigration (birth, death, birth, death...) is precisely so. With our activities of body, speech and mind, there can be no end to transmigration in the six paths. But how would we transmigrate if our self-generated actions ceased? Here, for the first time, this struck my heart, and realising the nature of birth and death, I grasped the essence of the Buddha's teaching.'[38]

Seven centuries earlier, the Indian monk Bodhidharma said:

'Delusion means mortality, and awareness means Buddhahood. They're not the same and they're not different. It is just that people distinguish delusion from awareness. When we're deluded there's a world to escape. When we're aware, there's nothing to escape.'[39]

Life is a constant of coming and going, rebecoming or

[38] *No Abode The Record of Ippen*, Dennis Hirota (trans.)
[39] *The Zen Teaching of Bodhidharma*, Red Pine (trans.)

rebirth and there is no birth and death of a personal self apart from in ignorance. Rebirth, then, is this changing phenomenon which the wise do not enter into. To enter into it is *samsara* (the cycle of birth and death); not to enter into it, is *nirvana* (beyond the cycle of birth and death). Everything comes to this midpoint of awareness, this poise and equanimity of the mind. This is a state which does not attach to joy or sorrow or conditions of any kind, but allows them to flow. There *is* joy, there *is* sorrow, but they are not clung to, and entered into, and so they pass by.

There was Siddhārtha Gautama, the man, the historical figure referred to as 'the Buddha', and then there is *being* buddha, *being* knowing, *being* reality at this very moment. There is no person involved, no individual being; just *being* as an ongoing experience.

Most of us have a mental image of who we think we are — name, personality, status — and we stick to that. But this is just our story. The Buddha told it differently:

'As one form changes into another, so is the mind born and broken up. Therefore I tell my disciples how uninterruptedly and momentarily birth and death takes place. In like manner, discrimination also rises and disappears with every single form. Where there is discrimination, there are living beings; outside of it there are no living beings.' [40]

---

[40] *The Lankavatara Sutra*, D.T. Suzuki (trans.)

Chapter Twenty-two

Being Awareness

We might one day say to ourselves, 'Okay, I'm really going to look at what I am. I'm not going to *think* about what I am or recall what others have told me I am, I'm just going to be very aware of what *is* here and now, for myself, in a direct way.' And a kind of determination sets in.

We then find a quiet spot, sit perfectly still, straighten the back, lower the eyes and attempt to centre the mind in the best way we can — just being aware of sensations and thoughts, not choosing what to be aware of, just watching, watching.

We want to know what birth is and we want to know what death is, and we also want to know what the Buddha meant when he talked about the unborn and the undying. So, we allow our thoughts to settle, the mind to clear, and in a calm, peaceful way — observe!

We witness sporadic thoughts, feelings, sounds, and

mental and physical sensations — we witness them but we don't enter into them — preferring to remain aware of the natural rhythm of life in an impersonal, impartial way, and peace sweeps over us — so good..!

But then the thoughts take hold once more as we wonder: *Am I doing it right? There must be more to it than this! There must be something else than just being aware of things coming and going into the mind, of sensations coming and going, of sounds coming and going and all the rest of it! But what is there other than these things? I can't see anything else. Where is the unborn? Where is the real 'me'? I'm not the feelings and I'm not the thoughts, but I simply can't find my real self!'*

And maybe in a sort of desperation we conclude:

I must be doing this all wrong. I need someone to help me. I need a guru to show me how to find my real 'self'. Maybe I should go to India..?' We then plan a strategy for finding out who or what we really are.

This is the mind getting carried away again by a medley of proliferating thoughts; this is us evading the issue, turning away from the reality of the present moment, forgetting what we are trying to do and getting caught up in our old mental habits of thinking, planning, dreaming and struggling to reach a goal. We have not stayed free of those mental proliferations long enough to observe the full picture, to see not only what comes and goes, but also the awareness behind it, beyond it.

Awareness has no form and does not move, so we tend not to notice it. When we become still and look at whatever is taking place, all we see is the transitory, the movements of thoughts and feelings, the world of birth and death.

There is something which the Buddha recognised under that tree two and a half thousand years ago — and which many had recognised before him — which does not come and go, something so close we don't usually notice it, something we have not awoken to — a nameless reality which is here and now.

It is here but we don't see it. Why not? Because we *are* what we are trying to see; we *are* the seeing itself, the awareness itself. Thoughts and feelings are 'things' to be aware of, but awareness is not a 'thing', so naturally it cannot be seen in the same way. A switch in consciousness has to be made. Not only do we have to *be* aware, we have to *know* awareness as well; we have to recognise that *we are awareness — that awareness is truly what we are.*

Chapter Twenty-three

The Essence of Seeing

We know that the re-becoming process is an actuality because we can see it. We know that our thoughts relentlessly switch from one to another, our hair slowly turns grey, our faces gradually wrinkle with age, even the rocks erode, albeit ever so slowly. We know and see impermanence, and we know and see the birth and death of beings, but can we know that which is *not* subject to birth and death?

A certain king, Prasenajit, once asked the Buddha to explain what he meant by birthlessness and deathlessness.

'Great King,' said the Buddha, 'is your body permanent and indestructible like a diamond, or does it change and decay?'

'My body will decay and will be destroyed,' said the King.

'But you have not yet died, so how do you know that your body will be destroyed?'

'I observe that it changes without a moment's pause and is bound to "go out" like a fire that gradually burns out and will be reduced to nothing.'

'You are old now,' said the Buddha, 'but how do you look compared to when you were a child?'

'My skin glowed, I was full of vigour. Now I grow thin, my spirits are dull, my hair is white and my face wrinkled. These imperceptible changes have been taking place in every decade, but when I look into it closely, I see that they have also been occurring yearly, and not only yearly, but monthly and daily and in each moment of thought. That is why I know that my body is destined to final destruction.'

'Great King, you observe this ceaseless change and know that you will die, but do you know that when you do, there is that which is in your body that does not die?'

'I really do *not* know that.'

'I will now show you the self-nature which is beyond birth and death. How old were you when you first saw the river Ganges?'

'My mother took me there when I was three. As we crossed the river, I can remember it was called the Ganges.'

'When you saw the Ganges at three, was its water the same as it was when you were thirteen?'

'It was the same when I was three and thirteen, and still is now that I'm sixty-two.'

'Today when you see the Ganges, do you notice that your seeing is "old" now whilst it was "young" then?'

'It has always been the same.'

'Great King, though your face is wrinkled, the nature of this essence of seeing is not wrinkled. Therefore, that which is wrinkled changes, and that which is free from wrinkles is unchanging. The changing is subject to destruction, whereas the unchanging fundamentally is beyond birth and death. How can it be subject to birth and death?[41]

The Buddha spoke of when he was first 'searching for the incomparable, matchless path to peace,' and said that although he was liable to birth because of self, liable to ageing, decay, disease, and sorrow because of self, he sought truth amongst what was also liable to these things. Then it occurred to him: *Suppose that I, knowing the peril in what is liable to birth and death because of self, should seek the unborn, unageing, unailing, undying, unsorrowing, the uttermost security from the bonds — nirvana.*

The Buddha's realisation that he was liable to birth and death because of 'self' was the turning point in his search. He realised that it was delusion about self which brought anguish and distress.

Freedom from 'self' and freedom from anguish are two sides of the same coin. The one goes with the other.

---

[41] *The Surangama Sutra*, Lu K'uan Yu

When our minds open to this immortal moment, therefore, there is no anguishing about anything, and questions such as: *Am I now? Was I in the past? Will I be in the future?* do not arise.

Bodies come into being, decay and die. The centre of our being, however, does not come into being and die. There is something which is unmoving and unchanging. Can we awaken to it? If we can, we shall have no doubts that the essence of what we are is unborn, and so is this moment — it neither comes from anywhere nor goes anywhere. This moment *now*, we shall realise in simple awareness, is beyond all conditions, immortal and indestructible.

We know experientially that there is just the wonder of the moment, we know it but not necessarily consciously. The point is to bring it to consciousness. That is the job we set ourselves when embarking upon the journey of our lives.

We live in *this* immortal moment that has no boundaries; it is as vast as space, but we think that something called 'time' is passing by. Birth into delusion takes place, and it takes place many, many times — delusive birth into delusive time.

Chapter Twenty-four

Thus Come

After his enlightenment Siddhārtha referred to himself as the *Tathagata*: meaning 'thus come' or 'being thus'; that which is not involved in becoming, abiding or passing away. Being awakened is not being 'an awakened person', it is just *being* — thus!

In 'thusness' there is no identifiable person, no 'me', no sense of having acquired anything or having lost anything; it is simply that at this moment, the 'Unborn Buddha Mind' — as Zen Master Bankei called it — is recognised, and all suffering ceases, leaving the perfection of just 'being', 'knowing' — thus!

Since the Unborn Buddha Mind is marvellously illuminating, it has not so much as a hair's breadth of any selfish bias, so it adapts itself freely, and as it encounters different sorts of circumstances, thoughts sporadically pop up. That's all right so long as you simply don't get involved with them. But if you do get involved with thoughts and go on developing them, you won't be able to stop, and then you'll obscure the marvellously illuminating function of the Buddha Mind and create delusions. On the other hand, since from the start the Buddha Mind is marvellously illuminating, readily illumining and distinguishing all things, when you hate and loathe those deluded thoughts that come up and try to stop them, you get caught up in stopping them and create a duality between the one who is doing the stopping and that which is being stopped. If you try to stop thought with thought, there will never be an end to it. It's just like trying to wash away blood with blood.[42]

When the Unborn Buddha Mind is recognised, we face life head on, we understand that we are not going anywhere or trying to reach a goal, or on a course leading to any kind of gain. This moment is everything and has everything. There is a Zen saying: *Gaining is delusion; losing is enlightenment.*

Kosho Uchiyama explained it like this:

In the ordinary human framework, we are always trying to fulfil our desires. We're satisfied only when all our desires are fulfilled. In Buddhism, though, it's just the opposite: It's important for us to leave our desires alone, without trying to fulfil

---

[42] *Bankei Zen*, Peter Haskel

them. If we push this one step further — gaining is delusion, losing is enlightenment — then we're talking about active participation in loss.[43]

When the Buddha was asked what he gained from enlightenment, he replied, 'I attained absolutely nothing from full and perfect enlightenment.' We might wonder whether it is worth it, then, if we don't get anything! But it is the loss that is the important thing here; not the loss of anything worth having, just the loss of anguishing, all that mental suffering, all those deluded states of mind. When all that is gone the mind is liberated.

When the unspoilt, ever-present, marvellously illuminating, unborn, undying, Buddha Mind is recognised, there is no discontent and suffering, and the realisation dawns that *concepts* about who or what we are have little to do with the *reality* of what we are. Indeed, there isn't a 'what we are', and it is like putting down a heavy weight — such a relief!

Once the Unborn Buddha Mind is recognised, the realisation also dawns that it was there from the very beginning — no gain, no loss, merely waking up from the dream.

---

[43] *Opening the Hand of Thought*, Kosho Uchiyama

Chapter Twenty-five

Not Beyond Yourself

The words: 'I am the All-seeing, All-knowing One,' which the Buddha spoke, means something like: *It is possible to see beyond the thinking mind, beyond views, opinions and concepts. I have done it and you can do it too if you wish. There is no 'I' or 'you', of course, and this is to be understood before such statements can be made!* And his teaching was always an invitation to: *Come and see for yourself. Walk the path. Do away with the suffering that you unnecessarily put yourself through.*

The Buddha pointed directly to the mind as the place in which to 'come and see'. Never did he refer to a physical path; never did he teach that one must go to a particular place, follow a particular set of rules or perform rituals. He did set up the Bhikkhu and Bhikkhuni Sangha (order of monks and nuns) and many rules *(vinaya)* developed around that community. The *vinaya* is related to living harmoniously with other members of the community and to the wider community, as well as keeping a strict moral code.[44] For those who want to devote themselves to meditation and contemplation, undertaking such a disciplined way of life can be enormously beneficial. The Buddha made it clear, however, that attachment to rules and rituals is a fetter, a hindrance to awakening.

We do not need to go to the places the Buddha passed through in India, therefore, nor do we need to emulate his lifestyle; that would be quite ludicrous and in many respects quite impossible. It isn't wrong to go to India, of course, or live more or less as the Buddha lived if that is the way it turns out for us, but it is foolish to copy others, even someone such as he, thinking that that will awaken us.

We have our own karma, our own past to live through, and the conditions of our lives will be unique according to that. The inner path, on the other hand, is the spiritual one, and it is a well trodden, familiar and ancient road.

Buddhism is a teaching that guides one to becoming conscious of something that we have always known but

---

[44] All Buddhists are expected to adhere to at least five precepts, but these are aspirations rather than rules. One undertakes to refrain from harming any living being, from taking that which is not freely given, from sexual misconduct, from false, malicious or harsh speech and foolish chatter, and from taking alcohol or recreational drugs which cloud the mind.

somehow ignored; it is beyond birth and death and beyond the conditions of the world; it is the truth of birthlessness and deathlessness, the truth of 'being' as a verb rather than 'being' as a noun.

Walking is experienced, talking is experienced, thinking is experienced, breathing is experienced. 'Knowing' those experiences is also experienced. Recognising the nature of that 'knowing' is where enlightenment lies.

Zen Master Bodhidharma taught that those who seek the Way do not look beyond themselves; they know that the mind is the Way. But when they find the mind, they find nothing, and when they find the Way they find nothing.[45]

The 'self' that we thought we were — that vague something which we might have believed lived in the body — is no longer regarded as a reality but merely a convention, a way of relating to others in the conventional world.

It is hard to recognise the extent of our mental habits, and it is hard to transcend them, because they are such strong habits, real addictions. As we become more familiar with the way the mind works, however, the more we see the connection between motives, thoughts, actions and the inevitable repercussions.

---

[45] *The Zen Teaching of Bodhidharma*, Red Pine (trans.)

The Buddha did not invent formulas, techniques or complicated descriptions. He travelled from place to place and talked simply and straightforwardly with those he met along the way.

Becoming aware of actions and the consequences of those actions reveals the principle of karma and rebirth (cause and effect) within our lives.

'Have your dealings with heaven,' says Trevor Leggett:

There is a saying: 'Don't have your dealings with people. Have your dealings with heaven.' If you have your dealings with people as they are, you will be entangled in like and dislike. Have your dealings with heaven, with space, and there is heaven in them, heaven in yourself.

Don't have your dealings with the clouds. Have your dealings with the sky. The clouds are the sky frowning, so to speak. There used to be an old song:

'Painting the Clouds with Sunshine'. Well, this is the opposite of the Buddhist training which is not trying to paint virtues onto something basically deluded, but is trying to dissolve delusions. There is a Japanese poem:

'The clouds are clearing up and soon there will be light' — don't think like this. From the very beginning, in the sky, there has been the bright moon.

So, it is not painting; it is clearing: Don't have your dealings with the clouds. Have your dealings with heaven. Don't have your dealings with the clouds in the people and in yourself, but have your dealings with the heaven which is shining in the people and in your own heart.[46]

When we see how we cling to desire for the things we want, and when we fully comprehend that the clinging itself brings anguish, worry and conflict, it begins to dawn on us that the best thing to do is desist from such a fruitless occupation.

Each moment lived *without* clinging — whether it be to an idea, an object, a person, or anything — is a moment *without* anguish. When we truly see that, we also see that that is where liberation lies, liberation from sorrow. This is a simple truth that many of us consistently disregard, though instinctively we might know it to be true.

---

[46] From a talk given by Trevor Leggett in 1987.

Chapter Twenty-six

Who Would Have Thought!

The Buddha taught that the birth and death of 'self' is a delusion; whilst the birth and death of mental activity, form, feeling, and perception, is the reality of changing phenomena. Change manifests as things coming and going, as the birth and death of beings; it is what we observe in daily life, and it is what the Buddha referred to as the life span of beings.

We can see that the 'me' of ten years ago is different from this 'me' now, and yet something inside us might feel exactly the same. The body, feelings, perceptions and mental activity are completely different, completely new — that is clear — but the knowing of these things, the *thus-ness* of the moment, has never changed; time has not passed as an actual experience and 'what-I-am-to-myself' has not come or gone either.

Waking up to the way things are in this living

moment is simple yet awesome. Hui Neng saw the essence of mind very early in his spiritual quest. He said:

> 'Who would have thought that the essence of mind is intrinsically pure! Who would have thought that the essence of mind is intrinsically free from becoming and annihilation! Who would have thought that the essence of mind is intrinsically self-sufficient! Who would have thought that the essence of mind is intrinsically free from change! Who would have thought that all things are the manifestation of the essence of mind!'[47]

Later in life Hui Neng taught that when we are able to follow truth on all occasions and when wisdom always rises in our minds, we can hold aloof from enlighten-ment as well as from ignorance; we can do away with truth as well as falsehood.

---

[47] *The Sutra of Hui Neng*, Wong Mou-Lam (trans.)

Chapter Twenty-seven

The Truth of Mystery

Questioning my grandmother's death started me on an inner journey which evolved over the years in a way I could never have predicted. Somewhere along the line — and it was a gradual process — those original questions transformed. It wasn't a question of losing interest in what happens to people when they die, but I began to realise that my questions were based on assumptions of what 'people' are in the first place.

I did not realise at the beginning that any deep inquiry into the nature of existence is bound to be from a place of naïvity and delusion, otherwise of course the inquiry would not be necessary. It isn't that our questions are wrong or are inappropriate or that we should ignore them. On the contrary, a question is a question and each one needs to be dealt with. And the way to do that is to thoroughly investigate it and eventually, hopefully, to get insight into it.

If we question thoroughly enough, our questions will not be satisfied with simple intellectual responses of an academic nature. In the final event, our questions — each and every one of them — need to be turned in on themselves. We shall then begin to see the flaws in our questions; we shall begin to see that somewhere along the line we have made assumptions about certain 'facts'. It is towards those assumptions that our inquiry begins to shift and our questions subtly change.

We don't really know where we are going when we set out on our journey; the path opens out before us with each step. Examining our questions and examining the assumptions we make in forming them is the way to proceed, and that is what is meant by 'meditation' in Buddhism.

Once our curiosity is roused about birth and death, the opportunity arises for an investigation into what lies beyond the surface of the mind. As we learn to recognise assumptions and drop them, we begin to face more and more the mystery of birth and death; we begin to face more and more the mystery itself — not as the unknown, but as a living ever-present reality where concepts remain unformed. We become more conscious of intuitive understanding instead; intuitively we recognise mystery for what it is. Mystery becomes a way of life;

mystery becomes our path, or as Seung Sahn said, 'the don't know mind'; is a living 'don't know', a living mystery; that is to say, not a dead thing like a concept. Intuitively, we see that truth has no name and that trying to give it one merely turns it into a theory and kills it stone dead, and also kills any chance of our knowing it.

Physical birth and death is not an assumption — we can see beings coming and going — but the birth and death of 'me to myself' or 'you to yourself' *is* an assumption. That is what we begin to realise on the intuitive level. We might not be able to pin it down intellectually, but we can recognise it intuitively; in other words we can start to awaken to the mind beyond concepts, views, opinions and ideas.

At the beginning of the seventh century the fifth Chinese patriarch, Master Hwang Yan, assembled his disciples and said:

> The question of incessant rebirth is a momentous one. Day after day, instead of trying to free yourselves from this bitter sea of life and death, you seem to go after tainted merits only, merits which will cause rebirth. Yet merits will be of no help if your 'essence of mind' is obscured. Go and seek for wisdom in your own mind.

Hwang Yan tried to encourage a freshness of spirit in his

disciples and inspired them to find freedom from this 'bitter sea of life and death'.

The Buddha subscribed to neither eternalism nor nihilism and never tired of saying so. As far as he was concerned, belief in anything — and that included theories about eternity and annihilation — were simply beliefs, mere speculation, whilst reality was something else.

Without notions of past, present and future, without beliefs in eternity or annihilation, we are left with the unformed, unmade, uncreated, unborn — a boundless namelessness; the mystery that can be seen and known but not told.

Chapter Twenty-eight

Everything Speaks the Dharma

'The Buddha Sakyamuni[48] isn't the only one to have given Dharma [spiritual] talks,' said Venerable Song-Chol[49], a Korean Chogye Buddhist Master: 'Everything throughout the universe always speaks the Dharma. Even the huge boulders atop the mountains give Dharma talks hundreds of times greater than the buddhas in the temples.' And Song-Chol said:

> You're probably asking how rocks, boulders and clumps of mud could give Dharma talks. But if you come to understand Buddhism, you'll realise that you should listen to the Dharma talks that the boulders are always giving, albeit not in what we know as spoken language. And the boulders aren't the only ones giving Dharma talks. Even the formless, shapeless, invisible void gives an eternal

---

[48] Siddhārtha Gautama, the historical Buddha.
[49] A Korean Son (Zen) monk of the Chogye tradition (1912-1993)

Dharma talk. Once you understand this, you'll realise that there isn't a thing anywhere that isn't giving Dharma talks or performing Buddhist rituals. Once you open up the eye of the heart, you're not just opening the eye — you're also opening the ear of the heart. And then you can hear the Dharma talks that the boulders are giving. This is what we call 'Dharma talks by the inanimate'.[50]

Intuitively we can feel life. When we communicate simply by speaking and listening to people, we might ignore the language of the universe. Human beings tend to be on the rather arrogant side, thinking that we are more intelligent than any other being and anything else. Intellectual we might be, but wise and compassionate is not something we can take for granted. When we see beyond the limited perspective of 'self', there are no divisions anywhere. All things are nature, and communication can take place on any level.

Tao Sheng, a Chinese monk of the fifth century made reference once to going into the mountains and imparting the Dharma teachings to the rocks. It followed an occasion when he mentioned to his fellow monks that all beings have the nature of buddha regardless of how little their faith is. The monks didn't agree with him and they

---

[50] *Opening the Eye, Dharma Messages* by Ven. Song-Chol, Brian Berry (trans.)

retaliated with, 'He's crazy! He's mentally ill! He knows what the *[Mahaparinirvana]* Sutra says [which at that time had not been fully translated from Sanskrit into Chinese], yet he deliberately contradicts it.' They were so angry that they expelled him from the community.

Tao Sheng then made a vow, 'If my explanation is in agreement with the Buddha's sutras and the Buddha's mind, then in the future I shall end my life while lecturing from the Dharma (teaching) Seat. But if I have spoken contrary to the Buddha's mind, this vow will not be fulfilled.'

Then Tao Sheng went into the mountains and imparted the teachings to the rocks and ragged boulders. And when the rocks heard him, they nodded in agreement.

When the *Mahaparinirvana Sutra* had been fully translated into Chinese, the truth of Tao Sheng's words were confirmed. He was then duly reinstated into the community and took up his teaching role once again. And, to round off the story, one day Tao Sheng paused during a discourse and — just as he had predicted — died whilst sitting on the Dharma Seat. The assembly looked up and said, 'He has gone to rebirth!' [51]

All that is born must die, including physical bodies, rocks, trees and the ancient rivers, but there is something

[51] *Sixth Patriarch's Sutra*, Tripitaka Master Hua

that intrinsically *is* which is not born, something bound-less. It is on this level that we know we are not separate from 'the rocks and ragged boulders'. This boundless reality is not an object which can be seen with the physical eyes, heard with the physical ears, touched with the physical hand, or understood with the conceptual mind, but we can *know* it, we can *realise* it. And when we do, something within us wakes up as though from a long sleep.

From the perspective of the awakened mind, not only does the notion of 'self' disappear but also the notion of 'other'. In awareness we see complete oneness; the indivisibility of all things.

That is what these two Zen monks (Song-Chol and Tao Sheng) were doing; they were expressing the complete oneness of their experience.

Chapter Twenty-nine

Unborn and Born Together

Through awareness one begins to realise that birth and death are the principles of change and the vehicle of karma. We start to see the way of things and know the peril of getting caught up in mental and emotional states which disturb the natural clarity of mind.

The unborn and the born go together; one is the other. Becoming aware of these two aspects of reality simultaneously is an important insight.

Our daily lives are full of ups and downs, twists and turns, rights and wrongs, hopes, wishes, fears, griefs, joys and sorrows. That is the way life is. Sometimes conditions are fleeting and sometimes they seem to last forever, but when we are in touch with a wider perspective, we can avoid being dragged down by any of them.

Freely, conditions arise — we can't stop them — and

freely, if we allow it, they go away. When we try to hang on to conditions, change them or seek to be rid of them, that is when we enter the karmic cycle, become a person, create a cause and receive an effect.

Whilst we are, in a sense, born into this world, we are also unborn. Buddhism is about becoming conscious of that unborn aspect whilst not rejecting the born. Conditions are not a delusion, but thinking they are permanent or personal *is*.

Not only notions about the self, but also of space and time are seen as part of the delusion. Zen Master Hui Neng told his disciples once, that even if they were a thousand miles from him, if at the same time they realised their essence of mind, it would be as if they were in his very presence. The place he was talking about was not a spot on the map but the vast, timeless, no-place of the moment.

He continued by saying that should people be unable to realise their own essential nature, even though they might be facing him, they would really be a thousand miles away.[52]

When old friends meet after many years apart they are often heard to say, 'It's as if no time at all has passed.' The face opposite looks that bit older, of course,

---

[52] *The Sutra of Hui Neng,* Wong Mou-Lam (trans.)

but it is possible to discuss events even after decades as though they happened just a few hours ago.

In the conventional sense, of course, time does pass. A measure of the calendar is marked off, the hands of the clock go round — and we call that 'time'. The same with space: distances are travelled because the scenery changes — and we call that 'space'. We also identify with the face in the mirror, the picture in the passport, and the sound of that familiar name — and we call that 'me'.

In that sense we do move from place to place, we are individual beings living in the world, and we do exist in time. But simultaneously — and this is where we become aware of the born and the unborn together — we always remain where we are, here and now, in this moment, unidentifiable, unlocatable, birthless, death-less, timeless.

In one sense we could see 'time' as just the present re-creating itself; we could see that the 'here and now' is never left even for one millisecond; and we could see that 'our world' is merely a moving kaleidoscope of conditions.

The feeling between old friends that 'no time at all has passed since we last met' hints at timelessness; the occasional doubt about really being that person in the mirror hints at the unborn; and feeling that wherever we are 'we are still here' hints at the immeasurable. But unless these hints are contemplated, the significance of them goes unrecognised and are brushed aside as vague feelings.

When I was about ten years old, my grandmother said to me, 'I bet you think I'm really old, don't you?' and I answered 'no', thinking that is what she wanted to hear, but she ignored my feeble response and continued, 'Well, I don't feel any different to when I was your age. Inside, I feel just the same.' Clearly, there was some part of her which recognised timelessness and the unborn.

Remember You Are as You've Always Been

It is one thing to learn about Buddhism; it is quite another to practise it. Understanding in conventional terms and realisation in Buddhist terms are two very different things. Whilst the teachings can inspire the mind, inspiration alone will never bring insight. We need to actually put the teachings into practice for them to have any effect.

If you start to get worried because you cannot find yourself apart from the thought 'me', remember that you are as you have always been, and that you are merely trying to uncover delusion. Becoming aware of reality does not destroy anything and it cannot destroy what one essentially is.

When you see what you see, know what you know, feel what you feel, when you are completely focused on this moment and do not attach to thoughts, there will be no fear or panic. Instead, there will be the sense that a huge weight has been lifted.

To be aware of conditions and to be simultaneously

conscious of the unconditioned, the unborn, the uncreated, the unmade, is to refrain from being born into them.

'If it were not for the unborn,' said the Buddha, 'there would be no escape from the born. But there *is* the unborn, therefore there *is* an escape.'

Bibliography

Another Kind of Birth, Buddhadasa Bhikkhu, Sivaphorn, 1969

Bankei Zen, Peter Haskel, Grove, 1984

Basic Buddhism: Exploring Buddhism and Zen, Nan Huai-Chin, Weiser, 1997

Blue Cliff Record, The, Thomas and J.C. Cleary (trans.), Shambhala, 1977

Book of the Kindred Sayings, The, Vol. II, Rhys Davids (trans.), Pali Text Society, 1952

Buddhism Now, Vol. VII, No. 1, February 1995, Buddhist Publishing Group

Buddhist Bible, A, Dwight Goddard, Harrap, 1956

Buddhist Dictionary: Manual of Buddhist Terms and Doctrines, Nyanatiloka, Forest Hermitage, Kandy, 1970

Cutting Edge, Vol. 1, No. 1, Zen Master Seung Sahn, 1985

Dhammapada, The, Narada Thera, The Corporate Body of the Buddha Educational Foundation, Taiwan, 1993.

Dialogues of the Buddha (Digha-Nikaya), Part II, Sacred Books of the Buddhists, T.W. and C.A.F. Rhys Davids (trans.), 1959

Gradual Sayings (Anguttara-Nikaya), The,
F.L. Woodward (trans.), Pali Text Society, 1972

History of Zen Buddhism, A, Heinrich Dumoulin,
Beacon, 1969

Lankavatara Sutra, The, D.T. Suzuki (trans.),
Routledge
& Kegan Paul, 1932

Light of Asia, The, Sir Edwin Arnold, Kegan Paul,
Trench, Trubner, 1919

*Middle Length Discourses of the Buddha (Majjhima-
Nikaya), The,* Bhikkhu Nanamoli (trans.), Wisdom,
1995

Middle Length Sayings (Majjhima-Nikaya), The, Vols.
I, II and III, I.B. Horner (trans.), Pali Text Society,
1975 and 1967

No Abode: The Record of Ippen, Dennis Hirota (trans.),
University of Hawai'i Press, 1997

Old Zen Master: Inspirations for Awakening, The,
Trevor Leggett, Buddhist Publishing Group, 2000

*Opening the Eye: Dharma Messages by Ven. Song-
Chol,* Brian Barry (trans.), 2002, Gimm-young
International, Korea.

Opening the Hand of Thought, Kosho Uchiyama,
Penguin Arkana, 1993

*Rider Encyclopedia of Eastern Philosophy and
Religion,*
Rider, 1989

Saddharmapundarika or The Lotus of the True Law, H.
Kern (trans.), Dover, 1963

Sanskrit-English Dictionary, A, Sir M. Monier-Williams, OUP, 1979

Sixth Patriarch's Sutra, Tripitaka Master Hua, Sino-American Buddhist Association, 1977

Some Sayings of the Buddha according to the Pali Canon, F.L. Woodward (trans.), The Buddhist Society, 1973

Surangama Sutra, The, Lu K'uan Yu (Charles Luk) (trans.), B.I. Publications, 1978

Sutra of Hui Neng, The, Wong Mou-Lam (trans.), Luzac, 1944

Tao Te Ching, Lao Tsu, Gia-Fu Feng and Jane English (trans.), Wildwood House, 1972

Two Zen Classics: Mumonkan & Hekiganroku, Katsuki Sekida *(trans.),* Weatherhill, 1977

Wheel of Death: Writings From Zen Buddhist and Other Sources, The, Philip Kapleau, George Allen & Unwin, 1972

Word of the Buddha, The, Nyanatiloka, BPS, 1968

Zen Comments on the Mumonkan, Zenkei Shibayama, Harper & Row, 1974

Zen Mind, Beginner's Mind, Shunryu Suzuki, Weatherhill, 1970

Zen Teaching of Bodhidharma, The, Red Pine (trans.), North Point Press, 1989

Zen Teaching of Instantaneous Awakening, Master Hui Hai, John Blofeld (trans.), Buddhist Publishing Group, 2007

Index

Also available from Buddhist Publishing Group

Don't Take Your Life Personally

by Ajahn Sumedho
Edited by Diana St Ruth

Ajahn Sumedho, an American Buddhist monk, urges us to trust in awareness and find out for ourselves what it is to experience genuine liberation from mental anguish and suffering. He encourages us not to take our lives personally, but to look at the reality of this moment free from beliefs, views and opinions; and he refers frequently to his own experiences along the path:

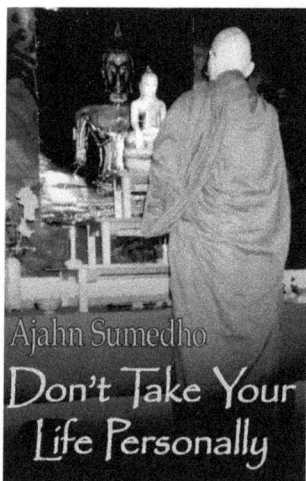

Mindfulness or awareness is knowing, isn't it? It is a direct knowing, immanent here and now. It is being fully present, attentive, to this present moment as is. On the other hand, defining mindfulness tends to make it into something — and then it is no longer mindfulness, is it? Mindfulness is not a thing; it is a recognition, an intuitive awareness. It is awareness without grasping. With this recognition, we have perspective on the conditions that we experience in the present — our thoughts, identities, and the conditioning we have.

ISBN 9780946672318.

The Embossed Tea Kettle

by Zen Master Hakuin
translated from the Japanese by
R.D.M. Shaw, D.D.
new edition abridged and revised by Diana St
Ruth.

Hakuin Zenji (1685-1769) was a great Zen Master. He was a man of extraordinary gifts, mystic and practical, strong and gentle, imbued with true compassion and with an open eye for the miseries of the human situation on all levels.

Though the earth is hard, tread on it softly!
Great things are destroyed by little things.
If you are careless about little things,
you will accomplish nothing.
Everybody — Wake up!
(Zen Master Hakuin)

ISBN 9780946672332.

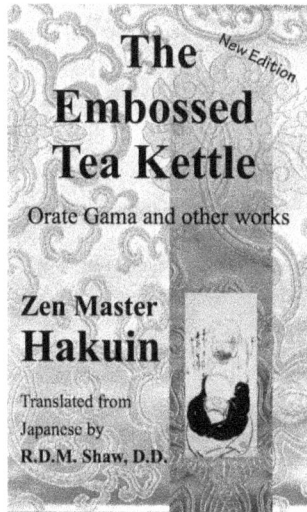

Zen Teaching of Instantaneous Awakening

by Zen Master Hui Hai
translated by John Blofeld
foreword by Charles Luk

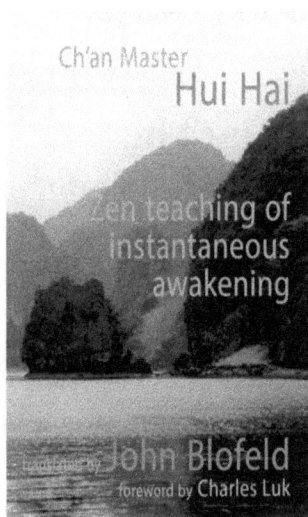

Ch'an Master
Hui Hai

Zen teaching of
instantaneous
awakening

John Blofeld
foreword by Charles Luk

Hui Hai was a great Zen Master of the same spiritual tradition as Hui Neng, Ma Tsu and Huang Po. His teaching touched this precise moment of truth:

When things happen, make no response.
Keep your mind from dwelling on anything whatsoever, keep it for ever still as the void, and utterly pure (without stain); and thereby spontaneously attain deliverance.

John Blofeld was a noted Buddhist author and translator, and was one of the very few Englishmen to have experienced life in Chinese Buddhist temples and monasteries at first hand before the Communist revolution.

ISBN 9780946672035.

Experience Beyond Thinking

by Diana St Ruth

An easy to follow guide to Buddhist meditation and the reflections of an ordinary practitioner.

Meditation allows us to see ourselves plainly as we are, as if standing before a large clear mirror. Nothing is hidden. It is like waking up from a dream into a new way of life completely free of all self-imposed restrictions and conflicting states of mind.

Have the courage to let a thought slip by without chasing after it – not clinging to thought, not rejecting it – the mind will open to a natural awareness. And awareness moves where life moves, not where hopes, fears, and wishes move. Come away from the wandering dreamy mind into the reality of the moment and cling to nothing. Be totally free. This is a distinct possibility for anyone who has the courage to trust life, forego the past, and allow the moment to be itself.

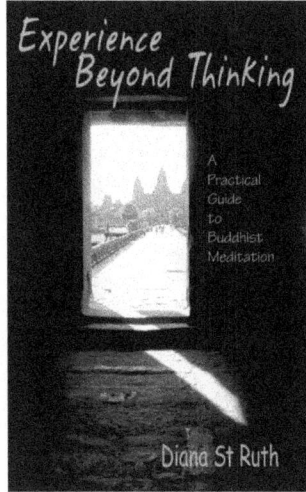

(Diana St Ruth)

ISBN 9780946672264.

The Old Zen Master
by Trevor Leggett

Stories, parables, and examples have been a favoured way of conveying spiritual insights and truths since time immemorial, and Trevor Leggett was a past master at it. He describes this as a freewheeling book: 'I am trying to give a few hints which have helped me and which may be of help to others.

Occasionally, a new slant, a new angle or a new illustration — especially if it is an unexpected one — can be a help in absorbing practice, study and devotion.

Trevor Leggett (1914-2000) lived for a considerable time in Japan. He was the head of the BBC Japanese World Service for twenty-four years, was the first foreigner to obtain the sixth dan (senior teachers degree) in judo, and wrote extensively on Zen.

ISBN 9780946672295.

Perfection of Wisdom: The Short Prajnaparamita Texts

translated by Edward Conze

The Perfection of Wisdom sutras are central to the Mahayana tradition. They offer guidance to those who wish to plumb the depths of their own minds and come face to face with the reality of existence by realising the truth of the Buddha's teachings on Emptiness and Great Wisdom.

The Short Prajnaparamita Texts were composed in India between 100 BC and AD 600, containing well-known texts such as the Perfection of Wisdom in 700 lines, the Heart Sutra and the Diamond Sutra.

Dr Edward Conze (1904-1979) was not only a great Buddhist scholar, but a serious practitioner. His translations are very highly regarded.

ISBN 9780946672288.

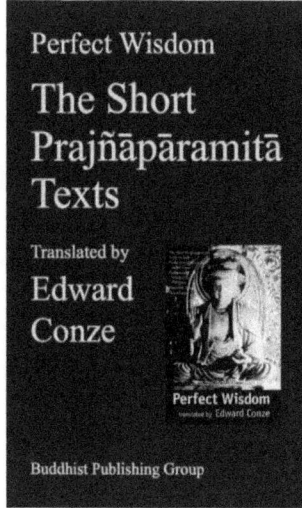

Fingers and Moons

by Trevor Leggett

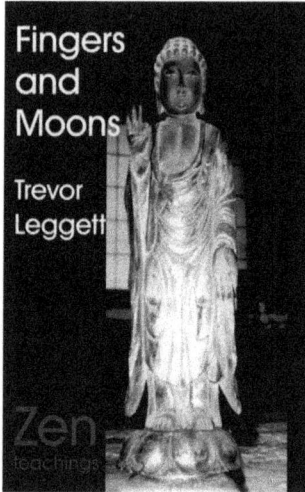

The well-known Buddhist phrase 'the finger pointing at the moon' refers to the means and the end, and the possibility of mistaking one for the other.

Trevor Leggett points out that the forms are the methods, but if we forget what the methods are and they become the goal in their own right, then our progress is liable to stop. 'On the other hand,' he says, 'there are those who say with considerable pride: "I don't want fingers or methods. I want to see the moon directly, directly... to see the moon directly... no methods or pointing." But in fact they don't see it! It's easy to say.'

Trevor Leggett (1914 – 2000) has been a leading writer on Zen Buddhism in the West. He lived for a considerable time in Japan and was the first foreigner to obtain the Sixth Dan (senior teachers degree) in judo from Kodokan.

ISBN 9780946672073.

Teachings of a Buddhist Monk

by Ajahn Sumedho

'Ajahn Sumedho invites us all, ordained and lay people alike, to enjoy the freedom beyond all conditions, a freedom from fears, from gain and loss, from pleasure and pain. This is the joy and happiness of the Buddha.'

(Jack Kornfield)

Ajahn Sumedho was ordained in Thailand in 1967 and trained under Ajahn Chah.

ISBN 9780946672233.

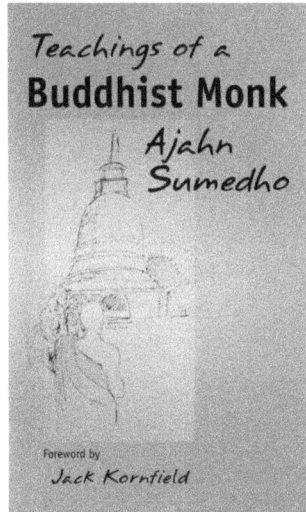

Find us online:

www.buddhistpublishing.com

Buddhism Now is our online Buddhist magazine, giving advice on how to practise Buddhism.

www.buddhismnow.com

And on

BlueSky:	@Buddhismnow.bsky.social
Facebook:	BuddhismNow
Instagram:	buddhism_now
Mastodon:	@Buddhismnow
Pinterest:	BuddhismNow
Threads:	buddhism_now
Tumblr:	buddhismnow
X (Twitter):	@Buddhism_now

www.ingramcontent.com/pod-product-compliance
Lightning Source LLC
Chambersburg PA
CBHW022022090426
42739CB00006BA/243